The
God of
Space and
Time

Space

The God of and Time

BERNARD J. COOKE

Holt, Rinehart and Winston
NEW YORK • CHICAGO • SAN FRANCISCO • ATLANTA
DALLAS • MONTREAL • TORONTO • LONDON • SYDNEY

Contents

Preface

THE GOD OF SPACE AND TIME is grounded in the conviction
that the Bible is relevant to modern man. When proclaimed
to or read to believing Christians, Scripture is not just a
record of what God *said,* it is a living word that he *speaks*
to a community of faith today. This word speaks to all the
critical questions and issues of modern man, providing both
insight and inspiration.

Such claims for the importance of Scripture have been
made frequently in the past few decades, as intensified scholarly research in the biblical texts has been translated into
popular writing, even into the elementary levels of religious
education. Unfortunately, not a few people have become
disillusioned with these claims. They have tried to read
Scripture, but have not found it to be religiously formative
for them; it has not seemed pertinent to the human questions
that arise in their lives. They have been bombarded with an
insistence on "salvation history" until they have become
bored by it. There is danger that the renewed interest in
Scripture will not survive the phase of novelty.

To say in response to this negative reaction that Scripture
has been inadequately or incorrectly presented, is no doubt
trite, but this may actually be the case. Scripture can be
treated as if it is little more than historical documents about
Israel and early Christianity which serve to clarify our religious and cultural origins; or it can be seen as a unique
anthology of religious literature, a treasured part of our

Christian heritage. If the Bible is no more than this, it might be interesting and even valuable to read, but could not one better invest his time in an investigation of the human and religious situation, not of ages past, but of men today?

This volume and the one that will follow it, CHRISTIAN COMMUNITY, RESPONSE TO REALITY, may seem arrogant in attempting to clarify the contemporary impact of Scripture. Such an attempt might well be arrogant, except for the fact that it is so extensively dependent upon a host of excellent studies of the Bible, studies that present in more detailed and scholarly form the relevance of the biblical writings for our own day. The "new thing" attempted by these two volumes is to bring twelve key areas of present-day religious thought into sharp interaction with the biblical literature, hoping to show thereby that the faith-experience of Old Testament Israel and primitive Christianity can still make a profound impact on our human situation.

Has God really done, or is he really doing, anything special in the lives of men? Is Christ as centrally important in human history as Christianity has claimed? Is the "new life" in which Christians have believed something that changes the actual experience of life? Does Christianity have anything to offer to the human struggle for freedom and dignity and peaceful serenity — or does it only hold out hope for better things in an afterlife?

What is religious faith? Even if it is possible to have Christian faith, and if there is some contribution it can make to human existence, why must it find expression in organized religion, in the Church? Is not an authoritative teaching Church fundamentally opposed to the freedom and responsibility of human persons; and is not a Church that stresses centuries-old traditions incapable of relevance in our rapidly-changing world?

Still more basically, is religion — a genuine relation and "dialogue" with God — even possible? What sense can it make to say that God talks with men, or that men can contact the divine as it truly is? And, of course, the ultimate question: If there is a God, who or what is he?

These are the questions these two volumes try to pose as honestly as possible, recognizing their importance today and attempting to confront them with the religious experience expressed in the biblical literature. This does not mean that the Bible offers ready-made answers to these questions or that the latter do not remain real and challenging, even when viewed in the biblical perspective. What is hoped, rather, is that the faith and experience of Israel and early Christianity can provide some guidance and insight for the task facing Christians today.

BERNARD J. COOKE

CHAPTER ONE

A God of Action

AS FAR AS we can gather from the evidence of history, man has always sought to understand his situation in this world and the sequence of experiences that make up what we call "human life." Our lives today are caught up in so many forms of this search for understanding of man that we scarcely notice all that is taking place: medical and biological research, sociological and ecological studies, psychological investigation — perhaps even more intense questioning in our literature and theater and popular songs. Somewhat more self-consciously, many have looked to "religion" in one form or another to provide the understanding of life that they seek: either some established form of religious faith, or yoga or zazen, or some very intense (and sometimes drug-induced) experience.

As we mentioned, this quest for knowledge about the human condition is not something new; probably it is intrinsic to man to live consciously and to have at the center of that consciousness an awareness of himself. Ancient man had already attained profound insights into the life of man in the world, even though the forms — poetic, political, artistic — he used in expressing himself may seem to us rather primitive. In the flow of experiences that entered into his consciousness, he discovered patterns. He understood that a basic phenomenon of the world about him, of the human society to which he belonged, and of his own bodily existence, was *order*.

Order and Chaos

This element of order pervaded all that man observed. Each year the seasons followed a clear sequence. Crops were planted and grew and only then could be harvested. Heavenly bodies like the sun and the moon obeyed an unfailing law of activity, rising and setting with predictable regularity. Most important, man's own life went through the stages of birth, childhood, maturity, old age, and death.

Not only physical nature but human society as well was characterized by observable and orderly patterns. Laws existed even before they were gathered together into codes; and innumerable customs governed behavior in family, town, and cult. Society was structured. Even though often quite simple, there were already established lines of authority; different people and different groups were assigned diverse roles in the social structure.

Quite logically, ancient man asked *whence* and *how* and *why* this order — and his interest was also practical. He was not only eager to understand the life that was his, but he was most eager to assure the orderly continuance of this cosmic and human order; his very life depended on it. Even the anticipated disappearance of the sun during the night was a source of fear for primitive man. One can only conjecture the anguish that must have come to him with extraordinary cosmic happenings such as eclipses of the sun or moon.

One reason why this fear of disastrous disruption of life's order was never too far from the consciousness of ancient peoples was that their experience contained evidence of a force opposed to order, the force of *chaos*. Difficult though it might be to describe or to grasp in any manner, the reality of chaos was too evident to deny. Besides the regular pattern of rains watering the earth and its vegetation, there were also the disastrous storms and floods. The regular pattern of youth, adulthood, and old age was often broken by the tragedy of early death. Disease, accident, war — these and many other experiences made it clear that the phenomenon of order in man's life and experience was balanced by the opposing force of disorder. This disorder was not limited to things beyond human control, like the forces of the cosmos. Into man's own activity, both individual and social, the influence of chaos somehow crept. Man found himself stirred by irrational desires and anger, torn by emotions he could neither understand nor fully control. In even the most highly organized and idealistic societies, undesirable forces — jealousy, dishonesty, corruption in various forms — entered and led to the society's ruin. Why human effort, in some cases altruistic and dedicated effort, should so often prove to be counterproductive, deeply puzzled ancient man (and is still a source of anguish for our own times!).

Primitive man's search for some understanding of chaos was painfully pragmatic. The forces of chaos were precisely what hung over him as a constant threat, endangering his happiness and health and very existence. Finding some way of removing or at least checking these destructive influences was necessarily the first task before him. Unless he somehow accomplished this, he would not even survive to accomplish anything else. Almost up to the middle of our own century, man's attitude to the world around him has been primarily one of trying to protect himself from the hostile forces threatening him: floods, drought, storms, disease.

Thus, in his attempt to discover intelligibility in his life and world, man very early noticed the intelligible element of order; but he also had forced upon him the irrationality of chaos and disorder. For primitive man life was a puzzling paradox, and to some extent life has continued to be this for men in every age.

Power

In addition to discovering order in his life, ancient man was increasingly aware of the omnipresent reality of *power*.

While power accompanied the manifestations of both order and chaos, it was a quite different kind of reality. If order consisted in some "pattern," power had to do rather with that which was "patterned." Power was the underlying dynamism that made things move and grow and live or, conversely, that destroyed things.

As ancient man experienced it, power took many forms. There was the heating power of the sun, the destructive power of flood waters or of a storm at sea, the sheer strength of the crocodile or of the chariot horses. Above all there was the mysterious force, fertility and life, which somehow coursed in continuity through vegetation and animals and man himself. Lacking any "scientific" knowledge of nutrition or respiration or reproduction, men in ancient times experientially linked the life force with blood or breath, with the planting of crops and the act of generation.

Despite these rather obvious associations of the life force with other elements of experience, the source and nature of life remained for men at this time a mystery. Yet they felt a compelling need to search out the secrets of life, so that they might remain in contact with whatever would safeguard life and guarantee its existence. For just as order was constantly threatened by chaos, life was unceasingly in conflict with the destructive power of death.

If man in the ancient world puzzled over the power he saw manifested in the world of nature, he was also deeply fascinated by the power he saw operating in his own social existence. What was this awesome force that some persons, like kings, had over other men? Why did the laws of the land possess an almost sacred force?

Even more basically, what strange power was contained in words, whether spoken or written? The ability of words to communicate among men was marvelous enough, but even more awesome was the word of authority, the verbal judgment of one in high office. This was effective word, language that made things happen, that brought events into being. And then there was the compelling voice of the charismatic person — the prophet, the seer, the shaman — who claimed to have a right to speak for divinity in one way or another.

Each man was, then, a focus of myriad forces. Some of these — the majority, if the man was fortunate — worked in his favor to bring life and prosperity and joy. Others hung over him as threats to everything he cherished and wished to attain or preserve. In this perilous situation, it was of impelling importance for him to gain some understanding of these various forces. As with his quest for knowledge about the phenomenon of order, his search for understanding of power was pragmatic. He wished to understand better how to harness, or at least stay in contact with, the forces that worked for his good. He wished to understand the powers of destruction so that he could more effectively avoid them or work to overcome them.

Myth

The study of ancient cultures shows us that man universally approached this matter of giving expression to his intelligible experience by telling stories, which we now group under the term "myth." We must be careful not to think that myths are necessarily crude and primitive. Nor must we think that all myths are alike; there are important differences between kinds of myth, as between the profound but unsophisticated Mesopotamian story of Gilgamesh and the sophisticated literary "myth of the cave" in Plato's *Republic*. In a sense, it seems that man is unavoidably a myth-making being. In every age of history, including our own, man has used his imagination to give form to his scientific or philosophical insights into reality. And while the scientific, psychological, or sociological theories we use to impose patterns on our experience of life may seem to the non-reflective observer to be totally "objective," they really are in their own way as "mythic" as any story employed by ancient man.

In any event, ancient peoples did use myths to express their insights into life and the world, and they attempted thereby to make human life more secure and manageable. Since, as we have seen, the phenomena of order and power touched both the sphere of physical nature and the sphere of man's life in society, it was quite understandable that men should have seen nature as being directed much as human society was. In the human situation men, especially the more important men, planned and plotted, struggled with one another and fought wars, tried to rule by giving gifts or threatening punishment. So, behind the observable gifts of rain and sun, behind the "punishments" of flood and earthquake, behind the orderliness of nature and the occasional disruptions of that order, there must be personal forces at work.

Whoever was at work in rain and sun and storm, presumably acted in a human way, even though dwelling in the realm of the "sacred." This homogeneity of human and divine action finds a striking instance in ancient Egypt where the Pharaoh, who himself was god in the midst of his people, lived an observable pattern of divine life. Moreover, by a process of identification that we today find hard to understand, he was somehow the personage in whom coincided great gods like Re and Horus and Osiris.

Even when divinity was not so sensibly present, as in the old Greek myths, men still imagined that the gods had their feasting and their quarrels, that they plotted against one another and strove to gain power among both themselves and men. Exalted though they were, Athena and Zeus and Poseidon — along with the entire pantheon — had their virtues and their faults. And the somewhat immature arbitrariness of their behavior was considered to be the source of the dangerous unpredictability of human life. Should one of the gods take offense at what he considered neglect by human worshippers, the persons involved might find themselves struck down by disease or the victims of a disastrous storm.

Or should the gods be feuding among themselves (which seemed to be the usual situation), the patrons of one god might find themselves suffering the wrath of his divine antagonist.

Man's early understanding of the "sacred," of the gods who operated in all the happenings of nature and in the experiences of men, was thoroughly anthropomorphic. Giving poetic and artistic expression to the fundamental "philosophical" insight that things which happened might be the effect of some cause — and if they happened in a somewhat patterned fashion must be the effect of rational causes — ancient man fashioned the gods to his own image and likeness. He made images towards which he directed his devotion. Or he told the mythic stories which he then enacted in his ritual.

But if the Greeks built an imposing temple on the promontory of Sounion and placed within it a magnificent statue of Poseidon, or if the Babylonians in their cult celebrated the cosmic victory of Marduk over Tiamat, they did these things not simply to give expression to their religious feelings or to glorify their patron gods. Rather, they sought to establish "contact points," situations in which they could somehow make their gods present and induce them, by gift or cultic magic, to be propitious.

For ancient man, then, human life and experience were not only permeated by the influence of the divine but dominated by it. Life was not primarily a matter of human planning and activity, although these did have their reality. Instead, the most basic fact of human existence was man's relationship to the gods. Life was a continuous encounter, beneficent or threatening, with the divine.

A Unique God

At first sight, ancient Israel's "encounter" with her god seems very little different from the religious experience of other peoples. In the beginning of their religious reflection, the Israelites thought of Yahweh as fighting against the divinities of their enemies and saw Yahweh's superior divine power as the explanation of their own military victories. As they gave expression to their faith-understanding of Yahweh, they were thoroughly anthropomorphic: they thought of him as becoming angry, being appeased by their gifts, seeking glory for himself, changing his mind. And the fact that they "discovered" his supporting and guiding influence in the historical events that actually forged them into a nation appears to be just another example of the universal human tendency toward mythic interpretation of life.

However — and this contention will require much more detailed justification — there is a radical difference between Israel's faith in her god and the mythic understandings of other ancient peoples. Granted the unmistakably anthropomorphic fashion in which the people of Israel thought about and described their divinity, this god Yahweh is strikingly unique.

At the heart of his uniqueness is the fact that he is looked upon as "a god who acts in history." Again, this would not seem at first to be a distinctive characteristic, since all ancient peoples attributed the events of their experience to some divine influence. In the case of Israel, however, specific historical happenings were related to an encounter with Yahweh. At an ascertainable point in history, not in the historical context of myth, Yahweh did something which brought Israel into existence or contributed to her development.

Granted that the exact nature of these "historical happenings" is vague, especially in the earliest strata of Israelitic religious tradition; granted also that the description of these events often involves an overlay of mythic elements and reflections of the cultic celebration of these events, it is still true that at the root of Israel's approach to understanding her god there is a basis in historical experience that is unique among ancient religions.

Leaving aside for the moment a judgment of whether the religious faith of Israel was justified, the observable evidence is that the faith of Israel reflects a distinctive approach to divinity. As we have seen, the divinities of other religions are the result of man's projection of his own manner of acting and thinking, and therefore of his assumption that things operate in a human manner on the level of the "sacred." "The gods" are a poetic creation of man, expressing his awareness that what happens must have some explanation.

But in the case of Israel, Yahweh is a god who is essentially "other." He has broken unexpectedly into human life; he has presented himself to a group of people whom he is choosing to be his own people. He is known most radically, not in philosophic reflection, but in the personal encounter of dialogue. He "speaks" to men, like the great prophets, who are definite historical figures, and through them to the entire people; and he expects a response through both cult and social life. The transcendance of Yahweh in Israel's faith is grounded primarily in his loving confrontation of his chosen ones, rather than in the superiority of his attributes and powers.

A Covenant God

It is easy enough to say that Israel's god confronted his people in history; it is much more difficult to understand how this could and actually did take place. According to the traditional faith of the Israelites, their confrontation with Yahweh involved certain key covenant actions on his part.

"Covenant" was not, of course, a new idea with the people of Israel. They would have known of such arrangements of alliance or contract from other ancient cultures around them. Two or more tribes could make a covenant with one another, pledging themselves reciprocally to perform certain mutually beneficial actions. Or a temporal ruler could make a covenant with his subjects, promising his protection and assistance (or at least his nonaggression) in exchange for their fealty. To see this kind of relationship also existing between a people and their god was quite logical.

In Israel's faith-understanding of the relation between Yahweh and herself, "covenant" takes on a rather definite meaning, though this meaning itself developed in the course of her history. Certainly there were contractual overtones to the alliance between Israel and Yahweh, but the initiative in the arrangement was always from the side of Yahweh. He it was that invited the people to this relationship with himself; he it was who set down the conditions on which the covenant would be established. On the other hand, Yahweh obviously had little, if anything, to gain from the arrangement; it was Israel that reaped the profit. Israel's covenant was, then, quite different from the ordinary kind of contractual arrangement.

So central to Israel's religious thinking was this notion of *berith,* covenant, that many of the leading ideas of the Old Testament are inseparably connected with it. In making the covenant with his people, Yahweh was choosing them as his special possession; this is the mystery of Israel's *election.* As the guide to fulfilling their role in the covenant they were given the *law.* In keeping this law and, in a special way, its cultic prescriptions, they performed the role that was proper to them, that of *service.* Fidelity to their respective covenant promises meant that both Yahweh and his people were just. If this justice was present on both sides, if the covenant was in full effect, *peace* was the result. One could extend the list, but this gives sufficient indication of the central role of this "covenant" category in the faith and life of the Old Testament people.

The Sinaitic Covenant

In the traditions of Israel preserved for us in the books of the Old Testament, the most ancient and fundamental covenant act of God was that which took place at Sinai. It is true that the traditions about the ancient patriarchs Abraham, Isaac, and Jacob already tell of their being specially singled out by God; but that period is looked upon as one of promise. The covenant had not yet been formally entered into; the people as such did not yet exist. That period still formed part of the prehistory of Israel.

The immediate preparation for the establishment of the chosen people begins when God comes to Moses, tells him his name, Yahweh, and directs him to lead his people from their servitude in Egypt (Ex. 3). Exactly when and under what conditions this exodus from Egypt took place is not perfectly clear. Even the exact role and identity of Moses is difficult to ascertain. The various traditions preserved in the Bible differ in their details, and have been expanded and "embroidered" by many generations of repetition and cultic usage. Underlying these traditions is some historical happening, a liberation of a group of Hebrew nomads from their Egyptian enslavement and their consequent wandering through the desert towards the land of Canaan.

In the course of this wandering under the leadership of Moses, the people came, as the tradition tells us, to the mountain of Sinai. Here Yahweh manifested himself to them in storm and fire, summoned Moses to the top of the mountain to receive the law, and then sent him back down to the people to invite them into the covenant (Ex. 19). Responding affirmatively to Moses' question, "Will you take Yahweh to be your god?" the assembled people pledged themselves to observe the law which was the condition of the covenant. Yahweh then pledged himself to be their god and formally chose them as his own people — and the stage was set for the formal sealing of this new arrangement.

As it is described in Exodus 24, the solemnization of the covenant took place at the foot of Mount Sinai. Moses built an altar, took the blood of the sacrificial victim, poured half of the blood on the altar (which represented God) and sprinkled the other half on the heads of the people, saying: "Behold the blood of the covenant."

And Moses wrote all the words of the Lord. And he rose early in the morning, and built an altar at the foot of the mountain, and twelve pillars, according to the twelve tribes of Israel. And he sent young men of the people of Israel, who offered burnt offerings and sacrificed peace offerings of oxen to the Lord. And Moses took half of the blood and put it in basins, and half of the blood he threw against the altar. Then he took the book of the covenant, and read it in the hearing of the people; and they said, "All that the Lord has spoken we will do, and we will be obedient." And Moses took the blood and threw it upon the people, and said, "Behold the blood of the new covenant which the Lord has made with you in accordance with all these words."

The symbolism of the action is clear: one blood, that is, one life, is now shared by the two partners in the contract; a blood bond joins them together in the most solemn of covenants.

Again, we are not certain of the exact details of this happening. The same chapter in Exodus contains in its latter half another tradition according to which the covenant was solemnized in a sacred covenant meal. But for all their differences in detail, the various traditions that eventually come together in the final text of the Old Testament agree that Israel as a people came into existence in an act of covenant into which the wanderers from Egypt entered at the invitation of Yahweh.

The faith of Israel is, then, rooted in the view that this divinity, Yahweh, *did something*. He and, in a true sense, he alone was responsible for their origin as a people. Other elements were recognized as playing a part in the constitution of this sociological unity which was the infant Israel — the people's desire to flee bondage, their need to band together against aggressive neighbors — but the agent of their unification was Yahweh himself acting through the mediation of Moses.

As the people continued their historical career, it was the tradition of the covenant action of Yahweh that provided not only a principle of continuing social unity but a basic principle of interpreting the various events in which they were involved. Their god had pledged himself to them at Sinai, and it was his guidance and protection that preserved and directed them as a people.

The event of Sinai, however, is only the beginning of Yahweh's work in forging a people for himself. As the narrative of the early books of the Bible unfolds, the wandering refugees from Egypt make their way through the desert, around the Dead Sea, and across the Jordan at the Jericho crossing — and the conquest of the land of Canaan begins. In the course of their journey towards the Jordan, the people are attacked by various enemies, discover their own military strength as they repulse these opponents, and come to realize that their god Yahweh is powerfully with them in battle.

By the time they come to cross the Jordan, Moses, the mediator of the Sinai covenant and the charismatic leader who has brought them out of Egypt and through the desert experience, is dead. The mantle of leadership has passed to his lieutenant, Joshua. And Joshua, in a three-pronged military offensive, sweeps all before him and conquers the land of Canaan, the land that had been promised of old to the patriarchs and to their descendants.

Actually, the possession of Canaan by the Israelites was a much more gradual and painstaking process than a rapid reading of the book of Joshua would indicate. A more careful reading reveals that the military success of Joshua was not total; this is confirmed by the book of Judges, which makes clear that for two hundred years or so the Israelites possessed only small pockets of land in Canaan and lived surrounded by more powerful neighbors. Only with David, about the year 1000 B.C., is the conquest of the land fully achieved.

There is no doubt that the tribes of Israel did gradually move into possession of the land. Though they were somewhat scattered, some of them even living east of the Jordan, they remained loosely united with one another in a tribal confederacy. At the heart of this confederacy stood their common tradition of covenant relationship to Yahweh, perhaps even some shared cultic celebration of this covenant.

One indication that the covenant identity served as the basic principle of unification is found in chapter 24 of the book of Joshua. There it tells how Joshua, having won the land, gathers the people together at Shechem. Those present include not only the group that had followed him out of the desert and into the promised land but also those inhabitants of the land who had decided to throw in their lot with the Israelites.

Confronting this assembly, much as Moses did with the people of Sinai, Joshua challenges them to join him in covenant allegiance to Yahweh. Should they wish to ally themselves with Joshua, they must choose Yahweh alone as their god, put away all the other divinities they had worshipped, and follow the prescriptions of Yahweh's law. Having made the covenant, they will be blessed by Yahweh if they are faithful or will be punished by him if they lapse into infidelity. As at Sinai, the people assent and the covenant is solemnized.

> And the people said to Joshua, "The Lord our God we will serve, and his voice we will obey." So Joshua made a covenant with the people that day, and made statutes and ordinances for them at Shechem. And Joshua wrote these words in the book of the law of God; and he took a great stone, and set it up there under the oak in the sanctuary of the Lord. And Joshua said to the people, "Behold this stone shall be a witness against us; for it has heard all the words of the Lord which he spoke to us; therefore it shall be a witness against you, lest you deal falsely with your God."

Whether or not this passage reflects a single historical happening, it does point to the historical situation which prevailed in the centuries immediately following the Israelites' entry into Canaan. Covenant faith in Yahweh, though it was at times confused (for the people were still at a primitive stage of their religious understanding), functioned as a principle of identity and unification for the tribes that were growing into unity as the people of Israel.

For approximately two centuries, the people of Israel lived

precariously in a loose confederacy, dwelling in small and somewhat isolated pockets amid constant harassment. The already dangerous situation worsened as the Philistines, with organized armies and iron weapons, moved eastward from the Mediterranean coast and threatened to wipe out the weaker Israelites. Defeated in battle, their central shrine of Shiloh utterly destroyed, the Israelites sought salvation by finding a king.

Their first choice, Saul, was not a happy one (1 Sam. 8-30). His short reign was beset with tension between himself and Samuel, the last and greatest of the judges; his armies were no match for the superior forces of the Philistines; and Samuel himself was apparently subject to fits of deep depression. Finally, he and his son, Jonathan, were slain in battle on Mount Gilboa.

Saul's successor, David, proved to be the savior that the people wanted. Not only did he defeat the Philistines and achieve the conquest of the entire promised land, he organized the people into a fairly coherent political and military unit. By the time he died in the middle of the tenth century B.C., David had united the twelve tribes into a national structure that lasted almost three and a half centuries.

Giving due recognition to the military and political genius of David, and to all the practical measures that led to the establishment of his kingdom, we must still take account of the religious nature of his undertaking. From all we can gather, he definitely saw himself called by Yahweh to lead the chosen people. And whether from political shrewdness or religious devotion (or a mixture of the two), he did place his own reign within the context of the Sinaitic covenant by bringing the Ark of the Covenant to Jerusalem (2 Sam. 6), where eventually it was enshrined in the temple built by his son, Solomon.

Certainly the famous "succession document" incorporated into the second book of Samuel (2 Sam. 9-20), deals with David's ascendancy and reign as an integral part of Israel's religious history and traditions. These chapters describing the years of David's rule are of great historical importance. Apparently they originated as a form of court annals during the time of David and Solomon, and were incorporated with only minor editorial modifications into the historical books as we now have them in the Bible.

For this reason these passages give us an excellent insight into the understanding of the Israelites regarding the origins of the kingship. The traditions surrounding the short-lived kingship of Saul reflect two opposing views: one sees Saul's choice as something initiated by God through Samuel, the other sees it as something merely tolerated by God (1 Sam. 8-12). The traditions regarding David all clearly look on him as "the Lord's anointed."

The Davidic Covenant

With David there is a basic reorientation of the notion of covenant, although this does not mean repudiation of the Sinai covenant by him. His reign, in fact, probably made a major contribution to solidifying the cult and the law associated with this covenant. But within the Sinai covenant dispensation there now arose faith in another covenant, one between Yahweh and the Davidic dynasty. In order to provide for his people, to direct them in their wars, to take care of the underprivileged in society, to make provision for Israel's cultic fulfillment of the covenant, Yahweh has given the people his servant David. Not only David, but his heirs as well, for there will always be an heir of David upon the throne of Judah — at least as long as the dynasty is faithful to its role in the covenant.

The heart of the tradition about the origin of Yahweh's covenant with the Davidic family is contained in 2 Samuel 7, which describes the promise that God gave to David through the mediation of the prophet Nathan:

> And I will appoint a place for my people Israel, and will plant them, that they may dwell in their own place, and be dis-

turbed no more; and violent men shall afflict them no more, as formerly, from the time that I appointed judges over my people Israel; and I will give you rest from all your enemies. Moreover the Lord declares to you that the Lord will make you a house. When your days are fulfilled and you lie down with your Fathers, I will raise up your offspring after you, who shall come forth from your body, and I will establish his kingdom. He shall build a house for my name, and I will establish the throne of his kingdom forever. I will be his father, and he shall be my son. When he commits iniquity, I will chasten him with the rod of men, with the stripes of the sons of men; but I will not take my steadfast love from him, as I took it from Saul, whom I put away from before you. And your house and your kingdom shall be made sure for ever before me; your throne shall be established forever.

David had proposed to build in Jerusalem a shrine in which the Ark of the Covenant could be placed and where Yahweh could be worshipped. The prophet, speaking for Yahweh, tells David that not he but his son, Solomon, will actually build the temple; but that Yahweh's blessing will remain with David and his heirs forever. The tradition contained in this passage provides the root of the messianic expectations that evolve in the next few centuries.

It is difficult to ascertain the extent to which Yahweh's action, his "intervention" in the happenings of David's day, can be said to account for the emergence of kingship in Israel. Even among the thinkers of Israel in consequent centuries this is a disputed point. But the texts we possess do clearly indicate that the Israelites exemplify again by their tradition of David's covenant with Yahweh the basic principle: Israel's faith sees her God, Yahweh, as manifesting himself to her in the events of history.

Israel's continuing belief in the divine election of her kings is all the more remarkable when one reflects on the actual historical development of kingship in Israel. The national unity achieved by David did not outlive his immediate successor, Solomon. After the death of Solomon, the northern tribes broke off and formed their own kingdom. This two-kingdom schism, the kingdom of Israel to the north and the kingdom of Judah in the south, lasted until the destruction of both by the Assyrians and Babylonians. And during their rules, the kings of both nations were less than striking examples of fidelity to the convenant. The Deuteronomic editors who later gathered together the historical traditions of Israel could find only two kings whose reign they were able to commend: Hezekiah and Josiah.

With the ascendancy of the great Mesopotamian empires and their conquest of both kingdoms, kingship disappeared from the social existence of Israel. In 722, the northern kingdom of Israel and its capital at Samaria were destroyed by the Assyrian armies; and in 586 Jerusalem, the capital of the southern kingdom of Judah, was sacked by the Babylonians, and the people carried off into exile. The north was never restored as a political entity, and though the exiles from Judah were allowed to return and rebuild Jerusalem, they never again were governed by kings.

One would imagine that the experience of utter defeat would have raised questions in the minds of the Israelites about the protection their covenant god, Yahweh, was giving them. Actually, a great soul-searching did take place at this time among the people. What emerged from this examination was a deepened insight into their relationship to God, and a repentant recognition that it was their own infidelity to the covenant that lay at the root of their disasters.

In light of the historical events of the sixth, seventh, and eighth centuries B.C., it is remarkable that the Israelites kept their belief that they were "the chosen people." Humanly speaking, there was very little to support such a contention: they were consistently defeated in their wars; their cities were destroyed and the populations carried off into subjection; internally they were torn by strife and dissension; and their religious situation seemed almost always in need of deep reform. Yet they did keep their faith in the reality of their covenant election; and when the opportunity was given to them to return to Jerusalem, a sizable group did come back to rebuild the city and its Temple.

The stage was set for the return from Babylonian exile by the decree of Cyrus in 538 which permitted the Jews to reestablish their cult and their community existence in Jerusalem. There was an almost immediate response to this invitation, but on a very small scale; the first well-organized resettlement, under the direction of Zerubbabel and the high priest Jesuah, probably took place about 530. However, the situation created by these two leaders proved to be a somewhat stagnant one; very little seems to have happened after a first burst of enthusiasm and rebuilding.

The Covenant Since Ezra

Around 450 the more thorough and definitive restoration occurred under the leadership of the governor Nehemiah and of Ezra (who is referred to as both priest and scribe). Life in Jerusalem is placed on a firm footing and the Temple cult is restored to full expression. In the ninth and tenth chapters of the book of Nehemiah we find described the solemn ceremony of reestablishment, in which the people and their leaders assemble to confess their guilt before Yahweh, to ask his pardon and the continuation of his covenant love for them, and to pledge themselves to him anew in covenant oath. What we seem to have described in this passage is the establishment, or reestablishment, of the great feast of Tabernacles, which in the future would commemorate both the people's escape from Egyptian slavery and their return from Babylonian exile.

We see here how the covenant mentality has remained constant even at this rather late date. The happenings of Israel's history are still seen by the people within the framework of their election by Yahweh to be his people; the disasters they have undergone are explained in terms of their own infidelity to Yahweh's covenant with them. Moreover, they see the covenant not only as a reality of the past, but as the key to their present and future existence. Judaism — the situation of Israel after the return from exile — is seen to be the result of Yahweh's covenant dispensation, just as the original tribal confederacy and the period of the kingship were seen to result from that dispensation.

Though we have treated only a few of the highpoints in Israel's history, and treated them very rapidly, this may serve to illustrate the principle that we are examining: namely, that Israel thought of its god as one whom she came to know through his guidance of her life, whom she "met" in his saving actions. It is noteworthy that the traditions of the key covenant enactments are attached to what were historically the principal turning points in Israel's development as a people. The origins of this people are foreshadowed in the promises made to the patriarchs: the actual beginnings of the people as such are linked with the covenant on Sinai. Their organization into the tribal confederacy and their first possession of the land is tied to the covenant ceremony under Joshua at Shechem. When the social structures change to those of national unity under kingship, this again is attributed to Yahweh's covenant guidance (in this instance the covenant is made specifically with David and his successors). And when kingship fails and the Jews return from exile to rebuild Jerusalem, the hierocratic structures of Judaism are again seen to be a translation of the people's covenant relationship with Yahweh.

By way of parenthesis we might add that this idea of a covenantal foundation for their community existence is still very much alive among Jews of our own day. Many people today, Jews and non-Jews alike, have puzzled over the identity of this remarkable group of people, and over their strange and often tragic historical odyssey. Is a Jew a Jew because of ethnic ties, or because he shares a special cultural heritage, or because he participates in Jewish cult and follows Jewish practices? None of these seem sufficient to explain a modern Jew's identification of himself as Jewish, nor do they explain the remarkable tenacity with which this people has clung to existence despite persecution and genocide. Among many Jewish thinkers today the answer to this question of Jewish identity is given in terms of covenant: a Jew is one who belongs to this community of believers who stand in covenant relation to the god of Israel.

The God of Israel

To return to the Old Testament period, we might now ask: If the people of ancient Israel did believe that they encountered their god in the actions of history, particularly in his covenant actions, how did they conceive him, how did they think of him? In order to acknowledge him in their faith and worship, they obviously must have used some other name or names for him; and these names would indicate the conceptualizations they made in thinking about him. Or when they contrasted him to other divinities, they must have referred to certain characteristics that singled him out.

Unavoidably, the manner in which the Israelites thought of their god, even into the later centuries of Old Testament times, was strongly anthropomorphic. After all, it is rather difficult for human beings to think in other than human terms. Moreover, the Israelites' growing insight into Yahweh's providential guidance of the cosmos led them to think in terms of his power, his wishes, his "eternity." At the same time, the ancient law of Israel against making images of her god kept them aware of the idolatrous danger of thinking of Yahweh in human fashion. More positively, some of the distinctive names they gave their god indicate his uniqueness in the history of ancient religions.

In many ways the most basic and characteristic definition of the god of Israel is: ". . . the Lord who brought us up from the land of Egypt" (Jer. 2:6). We have already indicated how this recollection of the origins of Israel in the events of Exodus, including the enactment of the Sinai covenant, dominated the religious traditions of the people throughout the centuries of Old Testament history. We need only read through the psalms that glorify Yahweh for his great deeds in the Exodus to realize how fundamental to the cultic acknowledgement of Yahweh this idea was.

> Both we and our fathers have sinned;
>   we have committed iniquity, we have done wickedly.
> Our fathers, when they were in Egypt,
>   did not consider thy wonderful works;
> they did not remember the abundance of thy steadfast love,
>   but rebelled against the Most High at the Red Sea.
> Yet he saved them for his name's sake,
>   that he might make known his mighty power.
> He rebuked the Red Sea, and it became dry;
>   and he led them through the deep as through a desert.
> So he saved them from the hand of the foe,
>   and delivered them from the power of the enemy.
> And the waters covered their adversaries;
>   not one of them was left.
> Then they believed his words;
>   they sang his praise.
>
> Ps. 106:6-12.

As Israel's understanding of her god broadened, the ideas of Yahweh's power and governance and wisdom and transcendance were attributed to this god who "brought us up from the land of Egypt." This denomination, then, indicates the basic "category" of thinking that operated in the faith of Israel when she identified her god.

Another aspect of ancient Israel's identification of Yahweh is reflected in the often-repeated statement, put in the mouth of Yahweh: "I will be your god; and you will be my people." In succinct form this states the covenant relation that binds Yahweh and Israel to each other. More specifically it enunciates Yahweh's role in the covenant: he will be the protecting and guiding divinity for this group of men and women; he will look on them as his own "chosen people," as the object of special concern in his providential direction of history.

In a sense, Israel is here viewing her god in terms of her own identity as a social group. Yahweh is *this* god whom they worship, whereas other peoples worship other gods. To this extent it might seem that Israel's view of her god is no different from that of other ancient religions, each of which felt that it had a special protecting god (or gods). Yet the case of Israel is not directly and basically the same, for the origin of her belief in such a protecting divinity is linked with actual historical happenings and *derives* from these happenings. One may question the legitimacy of Israel's faith, the objectivity of her belief that Yahweh was really active in these happenings, but for the moment we only wish to stress the fact that Israel's understanding of her god came precisely from such happenings.

"I will be your god and you will be my people," is not a statement that describes Yahweh as the "personification" of the people's destiny or national genius. Rather, it is a sentence that comes from the covenant traditions of Israel. Its use in any passage of the Old Testament carries with it clear overtones of these covenant traditions and for this reason it reflects sharply the basically historical point of view with which the Israelites looked on their god.

Another of the most basic and consistent attributes attached to Yahweh is that of savior. He is a "saving god" to his people. Not only is he explicitly characterized this way, but the main theme that runs throughout Israel's religious traditions and binds them into a unity is Yahweh's saving activity. He saved his people from Egyptian servitude and the threatening power of the Pharoah; he saved them from death by starvation in the desert; he saved them time and again from the military inroads of their enemies; he saved and restored them when their own culpability and foolishness had brought them to disaster and exile. As their spiritual insight deepens under the impact of the prophetic voice, they become increasingly aware of the way in which Yahweh saves them from themselves, from their sinfulness and frailty.

So fundamental to the entire literature of the Old Testament is this theme of Yahweh's great saving actions that we have become accustomed to refer to the sequence of events in Old Testament times as "salvation history." Certainly such a term, though not used as such in Scripture, is in accord with the general outlook and belief of the authors who expressed Israel's traditions in the books of the Old Testament. At the risk of belaboring the point, one can see again how tied to historical events the faith of Israel in Yahweh was.

Another name given to Yahweh from very early in the history of Israel is *Yahweh Sabaoth*, "Lord of hosts" (2 Sam. 6). There are clear indications that this title is connected with Yahweh's protection of the people in their military undertakings. Yahweh is the Lord of armies and powerful beyond any of the enemies' gods. The Israelites certainly looked to Yahweh for support in their wars and thought of him as a warrior on their behalf. In this respect the usage of Israel was not that distinctive, for many ancient peoples venerated warrior gods and looked to them for protection. Still the use of the name Yahweh Sabaoth fits well into the Israelitic mentality that we have been sketching, showing again that these people viewed their god in the light of actual historical happenings.

Yahweh is, then, "the god of Israel," but not in the sense of being the personification of the spirit or the genius of the people. His role stands in marked contrast to that found for the god of many other ancient religions. In Egypt, for example, the Pharaoh (particularly in the older period of Egyptian history) was looked upon as divine, as god living in the midst of the people. Moreover, he contained in himself all the "personhood" of the people; he alone possessed of himself a "ka," the principle of autonomous personal identity. Other people in Egypt had life and identity and destiny only in relation to the Pharaoh, both in this life and in the next.

In Greece, certain divinities came to be looked upon as personifying the spirit and destiny of one or other city-state. Pallas Athena, the patron goddess of Athens, was described in terms that typified the ideal of intelligence and wisdom that the Athenians espoused for themselves. True, this goddess is found along with the other divinities of the classical pantheon that one finds in various Indo-European cultures, and she is already mentioned in the ancient myths that antedate the rise of Athens to prominence. But that is precisely the point: As Athens becomes more powerful and culturally developed, the characterization of Pallas Athena takes on more and more elements of the Athenian genius and achievement. In a sense, she came to be the "first citizen" of the city.

It was quite otherwise in Israel, where, as we will see more fully, Israel took her own identity from that of Yahweh. Again, while it was a common pattern in ancient cultures for one or other of the gods to be the support of the social and political structures of society, the manner in which this occurred in Israel seems quite distinctive. To take laws as an example: In a culture like that of ancient Assyria, the laws were promulgated as the legislation of the reigning king, and a god was appealed to as the one who would bring curses upon those who violated these statutes. In the famous Code of Hammurabi, it is clearly Hammurabi himself who makes and proclaims the law, and only at the end is reference made to the god who "backs up" the law. It is clearly royal law.

In Israel, even though kingship functioned for several centuries, and even though the kings of both Israel and Judah derived many of their royal practices from the kingships that surrounded them, there is never any royal code of law as such. Instead, the kings were considered to have the god-given responsibility of enforcing the law that had come from Yahweh himself. Unquestionably, during the years when the people of Israel were governed by kings, there was a considerable expansion of their laws to meet the changing needs of the social situation. Yet this law was legitimated by assimilating it to the basic traditions of law which, according to

Israel's faith, originated with Yahweh and his covenant action at Sinai. Yahweh, not the king, is the lawgiver in Israel.

What all this seems to point to is that Yahweh played a role in the life of the people of Israel quite different from the role of "the gods" in the life of other ancient peoples. He is not identified in relationship to the people. On the contrary, they find their identification, both as a social entity and as individuals, in relationship to him.

Israel's religion is so dominated by the distinctiveness of Yahweh that one can characterize it quite correctly as "Yahwistic religion." And Israel's social identity can find no clear distinguishing base except the people's belief that they are Yahweh's people, the people he picked from among all men to be his own chosen ones.

What is worth noting, too, is the historical fact that Israel's identification of self in relationship to Yahweh grows stronger and more profound over the centuries. In the very beginning, "when Israel was a child," the relation to Yahweh was apparently seen in quite pragmatic fashion. Yahweh would watch over the people if they kept his laws, above all if they would worship him as their god. He had called them, elected them, and this fact stood at the origin of their historical existence as a distinguishable social unit. Yet he was viewed as an overlord and they as his servants.

By the time of the great prophets, this view has been considerably modified. While one must be careful not to read the literature of the prophetic period as if the religious leaders of those days thought and spoke like modern "personalists," it is still true that an important advance had been made in Israel's religious mentality. Yahweh is still definitely "the Lord," but he is also spoken of as a father who has raised Israel as his son (Hos. 11), as a husband who has espoused Israel as his own beloved (Hos. 2), as a mother who can never forget the children she has borne (Is. 49:15). The use of such figures of speech indicates that the process of achieving a self-identity by the Israelites was moving in the direction of a more personal relationship with their god.

One needs only to read some of the passages in the book of Jeremiah to realize how advanced was this personal attitude on the part of at least some of the Israelites. In the pleas that Jeremiah addresses to Yahweh there is a "holy audacity" that is almost shocking, as, for example, when he accuses Yahweh of what seems to be an infidelity to the promises he had made to the prophet:

> O Lord, thou hast deceived me, and I was deceived; thou art stronger than I, and thou hast prevailed.
> I have become a laughingstock all the day: everyone mocks me.
> For whenever I speak, I cry out, I shout, "Violence and destruction!"
> For the word of the Lord has become for me a reproach and derision all day long.
>
> Jer. 20:7-8

Such passages reveal how intimately and totally the prophet thinks of himself and his role in relation to Yahweh. Obviously, not all the people in Jeremiah's day shared his profound religious insights and attitudes; but we must not forget that his thought was preserved as part of Israel's tradition and was read in the later centuries of the Old Testament period as part of the synagogue worship. And not only did the Jews of those later centuries listen to such prophetic literature, many of the psalms that they used in synagogue and Temple to voice their response of faith incorporated the same level of deep personal relationship with Yahweh.

What was true of Israel's self-identification applied also to her people's perception of the role they were meant to play in history. Gradually they came to understand their function as one of testifying to Yahweh's name among the nations. In their Temple the name of Yahweh would be invoked with praise and reverence, his might and fidelity would be acknowledged, his claims upon them accepted. Furthermore, their very existence as a people, even the military and political reverses they suffered as a result of their sin, would manifest before all peoples the sanctity and the powerful mercy of Yahweh. Not only did Yahweh give meaning to Israel's historical career, in the last analysis all other nations would find themselves judged in terms of their relationship to Yahweh and to his people Israel. One finds such judgments unmistakably expressed in the oracles directed against other nations that are so prominent in some of the books of the prophets (e.g. Ezek. 25-32).

What Did Yahweh Do?

It seems clear, then, that Israel's religious outlook is distinguished by the fact that she thinks of her god in terms of the actions he performed for her in history. But for anyone who will examine seriously Israel's claim this raises the question: What precisely, if anything, did God do for this people? Were there, really, "interventions" of Yahweh in Israel's history? Did he exercise on their behalf a special providence, something beyond what he did through his basic sustaining providence for all peoples?

This question is, obviously, critical for Christians as well as Jews; both profess an acceptance in faith of Israel's traditions. Even if one is willing to accept these traditions, and acknowledge the expression of them in the Old Testament literature as the "word of God," the question still must be faced: What did God do for Israel that was special?

One can, of course, read the Bible in a very fundamentalist fashion and come up with a simple answer: God worked in a miraculous fashion throughout Israel's history. In the beginning he inflicted the plagues upon the Pharoah and the Egyptians, changing their water to blood, sending locusts and pestilence to destroy them. In their battles he supported the Israelites by directly confounding their enemies. He provided food and drink for them in the desert by direct miraculous action.

Granting that God can, and perhaps on occasion does,

work miraculously in human life, one must approach cautiously the Old Testament accounts of "miracles." First of all, the Israelites did not make the kind of distinction between "miraculous" and "ordinary" activity of God that we might be inclined to make. For them (as for other ancient peoples at a primitive stage of their development) any especially powerful occurrence in nature, like a storm or flood, was looked upon as "marvelous," particularly if it was unexpected. That such occurrences involved some "suspension of the ordinary laws of nature" (which is what we understand by a miracle) never entered their minds; this was not their way of thinking.

Secondly, the Israelites shared with all ancient peoples the tendency to attribute to direct divine activity many of the happenings that we have learned to explain as the result of natural forces. For this reason one can hardly appeal to the statements that Yahweh rained down hail on opposing armies, or caused a drought, as bases for justifying the unique historical character of Israel's god.

Thirdly, one must interpret any section of the Bible according to the kind of literature it is; poetry, parable, and straightforward historical annals are certainly not to be read in the same fashion. Much of Israel's traditional recounting of "Yahweh's great deeds" is preserved in poetic form, and it must therefore be read in that light. This is not to say that such passages are not rooted in historical happenings, that they are sheerly the product of literary imagination; it does say that one must be aware that the manner of describing an historical happening and the details introduced into the description may be quite imaginative.

A classic example of this principle can be found in the song of Deborah in the fifth chapter of Judges. Though this is a very ancient portion of the Old Testament text, and of great historical value because of the way in which it catches the spirit of the event it describes, the passage is clearly poetic (in contrast with the preceding chapter, which describes the same event in prose style), as it speaks of the stars fighting on the side of Israel, and of Yahweh marching with earthshaking advance to help his people.

Fourthly, we know that many of the Israelitic traditions that are now preserved in the books of the Bible were for long decades, even centuries, preserved through the cult that was celebrated in the Israelites' shrines. Central to this Israelitic liturgy was a celebration of the "great deeds" that Yahweh had worked for his people. Not only were these deeds described, probably with a certain addition of more impressive details, but we can surmise that there was some dramatic "reenactment" of these deeds — and in the course of such liturgical ceremonies certain elements of the cultic action itself probably passed into the traditional accounts. For this reason, as well as for the preceding three reasons, it seems that we cannot depend upon a fundamentalist interpretation of Old Testament "miracles" to provide an answer to the question: What did Yahweh do for his people?

One might approach the question from a different point of view, stressing the belief of Israel that Yahweh had spoken to his people through intermediaries, especially through Moses in the giving of the law. In this way, by the directions that he provided for his people, Yahweh could guide their actions, give them insights they would not otherwise have, and so make of their history something unique among ancient peoples.

But here, too, though the solution offered is more subtle, there seem to be problems. In what way does Yahweh give such directions to men like Moses? Does he actually make them hear his words? Does he give them what we might call special inspirations, planting ideas, as it were, in their minds? And can we safely say that all the things that the Israelites thought their god was telling them to do were actually dictated to them by their god?

There may be another possibility, which takes full account

of the testimony of some of Israel's great men that Yahweh "spoke" to them, but which does not demand an action of Yahweh that would be a "planting of ideas" in men's minds. This possibility would be that Yahweh changed the course of Israel's history precisely by making himself personally present to the great prophetic figures of the Old Testament and through them to the rest of the people.

Certainly, as the traditions of Israel indicate, all of these key figures who were the mediators between Yahweh and the people at the turning points of Israel's history felt that Yahweh made himself specially present to them, that he communicated ("spoke") with them. If one is going to give any credence to the Old Testament, one must take seriously this religious experience of Israel's prophetic figures. Otherwise, the faith of Israel is nothing more than a process of reading Yahweh into her history, a process of imagining that some god was responsible for what happened to the Israelites through the ordinary events of life.

In trying to give some intelligibility to Israel's claim that Yahweh communicated with her on a direct personal level, we might be helped by reflecting on the normal experience of human conversation. During such communication with one another we exchange ideas and experiences and enthusiasms through our words and our gestures. More basically, we communicate ourselves to one another: as a result of my conversations and dealings with a friend, he comes to know not only my thinking but me. He cannot formulate in words his knowledge of me, nor for that matter, can I in speaking with him find words that adequately convey my own self-understanding.

Intangible though this personal "presence" to one another is, it is definitely a real and important part of our experience. We know, too, that some persons have a much greater power of projecting themselves to others. In any group they have a power that somehow makes others very much aware of them, even if they talk very little, and that power can control the whole tone and atmosphere of a social gathering. Certain topics of conversation seem inappropriate in their presence; people are less careless in making superficially critical judgments; things somehow "look different" because of this person.

Though this analogy is most inadequate to interpret the Old Testament experience of Yahweh, it does seem to offer some aid in understanding the process we call "revelation." There is no question that Old Testament revelation is fundamentally Yahweh's *self*-revelation. Every other religious insight that the Israelite people possessed and transmitted to posterity in their sacred literature is derivative from their view of Yahweh as god.

There seems, then, to be some grounds for saying that what Yahweh did was to make himself personally present to the consciousness of certain key men, such as the prophets, and through them to the consciousness of the people. In itself this presence was achieved neither through visions nor through words, but simply by Yahweh "being there" for the prophet. However, this presence of Yahweh was received into the human awareness of the prophet and thus was conditioned by all his previous ideas and images of divinity. The reality of Yahweh challenges these preconceptions, for they do not "fit," but only gradually, through many centuries, are the anthropomorphic misreadings of this prophetic experience corrected. The understanding of Yahweh that any prophet shares as a result of his encounter with Yahweh must be critically appraised, so that one becomes aware of the elements of the prophet's own psychological structures that affected his religious experience.

Yahweh as he makes himself present to the prophet is a most "demanding" person. In the light of his presence the entire context of human life takes on changed meaning, a new and unexpected purpose. If one is to accept Yahweh's gift of self and enter into relationship with him, one must acknowledge this new meaning and purpose of life, and work to bring it to reality. Thus, Yahweh's act of making himself present is the fundamental "giving of law"; his reality "demands" a certain response from those who accept him in faith. These demands touch the cultic activity of Israel: the people are to worship Yahweh and no other divinity. The first commandment states this demand: "I am the Lord, your god . . . you shall have no other gods before me." Yahweh's demands touch also the life of Israel as a social entity; because Yahweh is who he is and Israel is his people, social injustice has no place in Israel's life.

Under the influence of this transforming "presence" of Yahweh, the leaders of Israel saw life differently than they would have otherwise, made decisions they would not otherwise have made, and entered upon a course of action that they would not otherwise have followed. In this way the pattern of Israel's historical existence was changed by the entry into their experience of this saving and demanding god. Many other influences helped direct the course of Israel's history as they did the histories of other peoples: threats of war, economic prosperity or poverty, "philosophical" insights into the meaning and nature of human life. But the unique element in Israel's life was its faith-consciousness of Yahweh; from it came insights and impulses that pervaded and changed radically the people's reaction to these other factors.

All of this does not rule out the possibility that God might also have worked in other ways in Israel's history, such as by direct interventions that really have to be classified as "miraculous." However, there does not seem to be any clear evidence of such interventions, and one can give a plausible explanation of Israel's history as a specially-guided process without having to invoke the miraculous. Even if there were such miraculous actions of Yahweh on Israel's behalf, the more basic and important direction of the people would still have taken place as a result of Yahweh making himself present to the faith of his people.

Understanding the action of God in "salvation history"

as one of making himself present to the consciousness of Israel's prophets is not a means of avoiding the difficulty inherent in explaining miracles. Instead, it may help us to grasp an important principle about the manner in which the divine saving activity operates. Having created persons and given them a personal destiny that they must achieve, God (to put it in our terms) respects the importance and integrity of human activity. Though he helps men, he expects them to build their world by their own decisions. He does not substitute his own direct intervening actions for the actions that men must themselves make if they are to achieve true personhood.

Saying that God intervened in the manner that we have suggested, by directly revealing himself to some of Israel's great religious leaders — and through them to the people — is, of course, a judgment that can only be made in faith. If one studies the Old Testament with a non-faith view, the most that can be said is that the Israelites believed this way and that their faith (justified or not) did influence the course of their history. But if one as a believer does accept the faith of Israel, then one can say that God revealed himself in the Old Testament period as "a god who acts in human history."

CHAPTER TWO

A God in the World

OURS IS A period in history that is often described as "secu-laristic." Large segments of the populace are truly a-religious. These people are not antagonistic to religion or to God; they are just indifferent, uninterested. They tend to look to man-made solutions for all human problems, and while they recognize that these are not yet totally satisfactory, they feel that nothing better can be provided at present. Religion, as far as they are concerned, has nothing realistic to offer mankind, except, perhaps, an ill-founded comfort and solace.

For the person of faith this attitude offers a challenge. What does religion have to offer human life? More specifically, what difference does Christianity make in the contemporary world? Perhaps in past centuries it was a force that helped to advance human development — but has not modern man outgrown the influence of religion and faith? And even if one accepts in faith the fact that God did intervene in the past through what we described in the previous chapter as the process of revelation, what difference does this make in human life and experience now? Is not religion at best a peripheral element with no significant effect on man in his present existence?

Obviously, any attempt to answer such questions must take into account our basic understanding of what it means to be human. In this regard contemporary insights stress very much what we might call "personalism." We are increasingly aware of what it means to be a person, to be gifted with thought and affectivity and sensitivity. Naturally, this is not a totally new discovery; previous ages were also quite conscious of the fact that men thought and loved and had emotions. But for a number of reasons — particularly the development of psychology, the perspective gained through increased knowledge of history, the liberation effected through increased technology — we have developed a more analytic understanding of the factors that compose our psychic and social existence.

As we view man, he is very much involved in the entire situation that comprises his "world." Though he is, most radically, a spirit, that is a person, he is unavoidably "spirit in the world." This description says much more than the obvious fact that human beings are located on this earth. What it indicates is that the very life of inner consciousness which man possesses as spirit can develop and find expression only in relationship to that which surrounds him — the world.

The very notion of person — a knowing self that reaches out to establish consciousness through contact with "objective" reality — indicates that the human person must live in relatedness to what is not himself. Only by the process of going out to others — other persons primarily, but also things — can he even become aware that he is a self, i.e. the kind of being who does exactly that. Man's relationship to his world is, then, central and indispensable to his existence as a person.

Space and Time

One of the most fundamental aspects of our human experience in the world is the fact that it is conditioned by space and time. Modern thought, especially from Kant onward, has been acutely conscious of this space-time framework for all human perception. Every event we experience takes place in this framework, which exercises a major influence on the way we interpret those events, and on the way in which we understand the entire pattern of our life.

Ancient peoples were deeply influenced by the manner in which the world around them operated, even by the basic geography to which they were exposed. In Egypt, for example, life was patterned into an almost monotonous regularity by the flatness of the land, broken only by the Nile, and by the completely predictable annual flooding and receding of the Nile. The tranquility that this effected in the psyche of the Egyptian people is reflected in the culture they developed. On the other hand, quite a different atmosphere of life was induced by the terrain and weather of the Mesopotamian valley, or by the rugged conjunction of mountain and sea that conditioned the life of men in Greece.

The cultures of man, both ancient and modern, indicate that men relate themselves in a profound way to what surrounds them spatially, that they find their meaning in terms of the meaning of the cosmos and their location in it. Much the same thing is true of man's relationship to time, to the sequence of events in human life. From the most ancient times men have apparently tried to provide meaning for their lives in terms of where they came from and where they were going — their origins and their destiny.

Modern reflection on the space-time experience indicates for us the extent to which this experience is subjectively conditioned. Men at different points in history or in different cultures have looked on space and time quite differently. For example, ancient cultures imagined space as "enclosed"; we today tend to look upon it as "open." "The world" is not an objective reality that always affects human experience in exactly the same way; as it enters into the personal life of any individual or any group "the world" is conditioned by the way in which that individual or group has been educated to look on space and time.

Thus, a precise interpretation of man's location in space and time plays an important role in the entire experience of being human. And if a religion such as Judaism or Christianity relates both space and time to the divine, the entirety of experience is placed in a sacred context. If both geography and history are considered to be under divine direction, man's life takes on a sacred significance, and religion has a most profound impact on human consciousness and activity.

To simplify our discussion, let us for the moment confine our attention to the spatial aspect of human experience, reserving a treatment of time and history for the next chapter. And as we look at the culture of ancient peoples, there seems to be two elements through which religion helped shape a view of the world surrounding man. First, there is a widespread inclination towards "animism," that is, finding the world peopled with all manner of invisible but powerful "spirits." Trees, rivers, animals, storms — all contain the presence of these beings, who are able to help or hinder men. As cultures become more sophisticated, naive belief in these omnipresent spirits lessens, and a drift towards pantheism develops. The world around man, as well as man himself, is seen as a manifestation of some all-encompassing divine reality. Perhaps the most striking example of this belief is found in Hinduism, where "the world" is considered to be the appearance of Brahma-Atman, who is both ultimate reality and ultimate self.

Secondly, there is a widespread practice of "discovering" or establishing certain specially sacred places which, interestingly, are often considered to be the "center of the earth." At these spots there is a special dwelling of one or other divinity. Most of these sacred places are seen to be "contact points" with the hidden world of divine forces. Mountain tops are often places to contact the gods above the earth, and caves are looked upon as openings to the lower world. Religion is closely linked with such sacred spots, and shrines are erected on them so that religious worship can guarantee contact with and protection by the gods.

In Israel the very nature and identity of her God, Yahweh, demanded a view of "the world" quite different from the ones we have just been describing. True, the Israelites never fully freed themselves from elements of animism in viewing the world around them, but as they developed a more clearly monotheistic faith they viewed such "spirits" as ultimately controlled by their god Yahweh. Besides, there is no trace in Israel's thought of a trend towards pantheism.

Actually, it is quite logical that there be no such movement towards pantheism: the god of Israel is Yahweh who, making himself personally present to her consciousness, stands opposite her in a relation of personal distinctiveness. As a person who speaks to the Israelites and demands from them a free response, he is necessarily *other* than them. Yahweh is Israel's god; he is not Israel. If revelation in the Old Testament period is what we have suggested — a mysterious but real religious experience in which Yahweh deals personally with the prophet — the religion of Israel is intrinsically preserved from both pantheism and basic animism.

This is not to suggest that in the faith and religion of Israel there is no "sacralization" of the spatial world. This world is definitely situated within the pervading and guiding influence of Yahweh, an influence that is felt in all places but concentrated in the land that Yahweh sets aside for his people, "the promised land." If we are to study the manner in which the experience of space is made sacred for the Israelites, we will have to examine the historical evolution of their thinking about a promised land.

According to the traditions preserved in the book of Genesis, the notion of a promised land is rooted in the promise that God made when he called Abraham from his homeland in Mesopotamia (Gen. 12:1-3). This initial invitation to "come into a land that I will give to you" is several times repeated to Abraham and to his descendants Isaac and Jacob. They do not yet possess the land, though they dwell in part of it. The full possession of the land awaits the historical emergence of the people of Israel through the exodus-covenant-conquest events.

We can notice in these early patriarchal traditions that the way in which Abraham worships his god is related to the land. The land of Canaan that is given to Abraham and to his progeny is not the "birthplace" or the "dwelling place" of this god; rather it is his possession which he can dispose of according to his pleasure, and he does so by giving it to the Israelites. There is, however, something special about this land, because it is a place of theophany, a place where God manifests himself in striking fashion (Gen. 28:10-17).

Driven by famine, Jacob and his sons leave the land of Canaan and migrate to Egypt. Despite a temporary prosperity in this new land, they can never identify themselves with it. They remain exiles, aliens in a strange land, surrounded by a people who worship gods they themselves (the descendants of Abraham) do not wish to worship. Geographically, they still think of themselves in terms of that "promised land" to which they long to return.

As their lot worsens in Egypt and they are subjected to persecution and enforced labor, their alien status becomes even clearer. At this point, Yahweh himself "intervenes." He comes unexpectedly to Moses and directs him to lead the people out of Egyptian slavery, through the desert, and back to the land that he will give them (Ex. 3:1-12). So, under Moses' leadership, they break from their Egyptian slavemasters, and begin their trek through the desert.

Whatever were the exact historical happenings surrounding the exodus from Egypt — and it is impossible to ascertain what these were — it is clear that the experience of leaving a fairly stable dwelling in Egypt must have had a deep effect on the people involved. Once more they were nomads, wandering from place to place with no firm geographical roots, unable to identify themselves in terms of a place they could really call their own. From one point of view this was a return to their tribal traditions, since the situation of the great patriarchs was fundamentally nomadic, even after their "settling" in the land of Canaan. But the unsettled character of their life was even more accentuated during those years when they wandered in the desert.

Though their view of themselves "in the world" was an unsettled one, the traditions coming from that period indicate there was an element which made their experience different from that of other nomadic groups of the time. They were not just wandering, they were "en route." At the term of their journey lay a place of settled abode, the land that had been promised them, to which Yahweh was even then leading them. In this way, they did locate themselves in terms of a definite place, and this place itself was seen in relation to their god; it was part of his dominion that he planned to entrust to their stewardship.

The event of the exodus, which was the determining experience for the whole ensuing life of Israel as a people, was, then, specified by the reality of Canaan as the "promised land." "Exodus" does denominate directly the "leaving" of Egypt, and it draws attention to the liberating action of Yahweh, in freeing the Israelites from Egyptian servitude. But the concrete historical happening that began with this liberation includes as its final state the entry into the land Yahweh was giving his people. Life for those wandering tribes that became Israel was a "coming from" and a "going to"; this life was cast basically in the image of a journey. It was, however, a journey with a purpose and a goal. Implicit in this purposeful journey-experience was a mentality that later developed as one of Israel's most characteristic attitudes, the view of life that we call "eschatological." In discussing (in the next chapter) Israel's view of time and history, we will treat this mentality in greater depth. We can note, however, that the attitude of expectation, of looking ahead to the fulfillment of divine promise, affects even the Israelites' understanding of the place where they live.

Israel's traditions about the entry into Canaan and the

conquest of the land leave no doubt that this was Yahweh's doing. True, the leadership of Joshua was indispensable, and the traditions focus on his activity much as they did on Moses' in the earlier stages of the exodus. Yet it was Yahweh who picked Joshua to succeed Moses, and it was Yahweh who guided Joshua in his military undertakings and in his work of uniting the tribes into a confederacy. To the faith-understanding of the Israelites, it was Yahweh who was giving to them this land he had promised (Jos. 24:2-13).

If the resumption of nomadic life in wandering through the desert caused in the Israelites a change in the manner in which they thought of themselves as spatially located, the period of settling down in the land of Canaan demanded an equally basic change of mentality. Slowly but steadily they developed into an agrarian people, increasingly tied to the land they were cultivating. They came to look on this land as their world, even though for two centuries they did not really possess most of it. They knew of the existence of other peoples and other lands, but this was the land of greatest importance.

One of the grave religious problems that arose for the Israelites in this new cultural situation was the fact that they were surrounded by an established agrarian culture which already "sacralized" the land through its own vegetation divinities. This Canaanite religion explained all the elements of an agricultural world — the planting of seed, the ploughing of the ground, the rains that made the crops grow — by reference to a pantheon of gods. From the charges made against the Israelite people by their prophets, we know that many of the Israelites drifted into worship of these gods, so that crops would be guaranteed.

Perhaps the most dramatic presentation of this problem occurs in the sequence of events described in 1 Kings, events in which the prophet Elijah plays the central role (1 Kings 17-18). Historically, this took place a full century after David, so we can see the persistence of the problem.

After futile attempts to convince Ahab, the king of Israel, that he should move against the worship of the fertility gods, Elijah takes more drastic action. To prove that Yahweh and not the pagan rain-god, Baal, is the source of the fertility of the crops, Elijah prophesies a drought — which ensues. Faced with the prospect of famine, the king begs Elijah to do something about it. The prophet's answer is the famous confrontation between himself and the priests of Baal on the mountaintop of Carmel. The priests of Baal prepare their sacrifice and pray to their god to accept it, with no effect. Then Elijah sets up his sacrifice, and it is caught up by Yahweh in fire. Having accepted Elijah's sacrifice, Yahweh then sends the much-needed rain.

Granting that the description of these happenings is somewhat fanciful, the basic message of the passage is clear: The authentic tradition of Israel rejects the "world-view" that sees the land of Canaan (now the land of Israel) as peopled and controlled by the pagan vegetation divinities. Instead, the sacralization of this place is effected by the providential activity of Yahweh. He it is who blesses this land and the chosen people he has placed on it.

The prophets of Israel are telling the people that, to understand their present world, they must remember Yahweh, who led their fathers out of Egypt and into this land, is the same god who controls the elements of nature. Thus the Israelites live surrounded by the merciful care of Yahweh, rather than by the powers that their pagan neighbors worship. He is the god who rules both the heavens and the earth, and Israel is the land he favors before all others. In this way, the "world" looks different to the people of Israel than it does to other people. Israel's world is specified by the reality of Yahweh.

Jerusalem, the Holy City

But while this basic reinterpretation of Israel's agrarian existence was gradually being effected, a new and different element became increasingly important: the central role of

Jerusalem. There had been for many centuries a settlement at Jerusalem, but it had never played a key function in the life of the people during the years of the judges and tribal confederacy. When, however, David finally completed the conquest of the land and temporarily unified the tribes into one nation, he took over Jerusalem and established it as his capital (2 Sam. 5:10-14).

The Old Testament traditions concerning the ascendancy and reign of David do not attribute the selection of Jerusalem to Yahweh. Instead, the decision was shrewd human judgment on David's part. By taking a neutral spot that was more or less midway between the two cultural poles of north and south, he did not commit himself to favoring either group. Moreover, it was quite strategically located from a military point of view. Even his decision to bring the Ark of the Covenant to his new capital, though it may have been at least in part an expression of his own dedication to the Sinaitic covenant, was a judgment that he made without any special "inspiration."

Later on, of course, when Jerusalem had become definitely established as the focus of Jewish life, its central position was attributed to Yahweh's influence. Since most of this later thinking centered on the role of the Temple, we can best evaluate it when we discuss the place of this Temple in Israel's sacralization of space.

To return to the influence exerted by David's choice of Jerusalem: We have here, even though it is still on a small scale, an illustration of the ancient urban mentality. Even though David's city was not particularly large, even by ancient standards, and though the primitive clustering of people within the city walls scarcely merits the name "urbanization," these city-dwellers began to look on life differently than those who remained in the countryside. Many portions of the Old Testament indicate that there was a lasting cleavage in the mentality of these two groups — those on the land and those in the city.

It was natural that life in the city should shape the way in which men thought about the world and their place in it. If those who tilled the fields thought of themselves in relation to the piece of land on which they dwelt and upon whose productivity their very life depended, it was logical that those who lived in a city like Jerusalem would develop a view of the world controlled by their urban surroundings and by the activities in which they were involved there. We know how thoroughly in our own day people from Boston or New York or Paris look on their city as their "homeland." This is their world, and it is quite distinct as a human experience.

In the urban situation, the manner in which agrarian Israel had sacralized its understanding of space was no longer effective. Yahweh as the ruler of the rain and of the fertility of the land did not "speak" to the urban situation. Certainly, the Jerusalemites of ancient times were concerned about the success of the crops, for their own livelihood and economic prosperity depended on the countryside. But how did Yahweh's reality touch the "secular" surroundings and activities of their city life and somehow make them part of a sacred world?

Two realities seem to have functioned in the mentality of the people to make Jerusalem a holy place and gradually *the* "holy city": the presence of the king and the Temple with its sacrificial cult.

We have already discussed the tradition, recorded in 2 Samuel 7, that David and his dynastic successors were the object of a special covenant. Yahweh, having promised his special protection to the Davidic line, remained in a distinctive relationship to these kings. Even when they were unfaithful to their role, they remained Yahweh's "anointed" shepherds of the people. Hence, Yahweh was considered to be particularly concerned about the king, specially watchful over him. Where the king was, there was a special presence of Yahweh. And since the king had established his court in

Jerusalem, the city shared in this more intensified providence of Yahweh.

Of more lasting and more profound importance as a sacralizing influence was the Temple. Built under Solomon as the royal shrine in which the king worshipped God, the Jerusalem Temple gradually took on a wider meaning and eventually gained recognition as the one place in which the sacrificial worship of Yahweh could legitimately take place. This centralization of Israel's worship in the Temple did not happen immediately. Other important shrines had existed long before David and Solomon, and many of these, such as the northern shrine of Bethel, resisted the monopolistic claims of the Jerusalem Temple priesthood. It was only in the century immediately before the Babylonian exile, after the Assyrian destruction of the northern kingdom of Israel, that Jerusalem's Temple gained fairly widespread acceptance as the unique place of worship.

But certainly in the later centuries of Old Testament history the Temple was looked upon as *the* place where Yahweh's guidance and protection of his people was focused. The Holy of Holies, the most sacred portion of the Temple area, contained the Ark of the Covenant, which not only stood as a constant memorial of "the Lord who brought us up from the land of Egypt," but which was also considered to be a throne for Yahweh. Not that Yahweh was in any way confined to or held within the Holy of Holies; his own proper dwelling place was "above the heavens." But he was specially present in this Temple. This was the preeminent contact point where he still spoke to his people through the proclamation of the law, and where the people could respond in faith and worship. Yahweh's presence to his people, his dwelling with them, found focal expression in the Temple (Ps. 84).

Here, too, in the court of sacrifice immediately before the Holy of Holies, the sacrificial worship of Israel found its most important, and eventually exclusive, expression. At the altar of sacrifice the covenant of Sinai was commemorated and renewed, the covenant relation of Yahweh and his people acknowledged and continued. Here, and extending into the adjoining portions of the Temple where the people were gathered, the needs and petitions of the people were directed to Yahweh in prayer and song.

With such a situation, it is not surprising the idea grew that Jerusalem with its Temple was the center of salvation, for Israel and for all peoples (Is. 60). While Yahweh was somehow present to all creation and controlling the destinies of all peoples, Jerusalem alone was his dwelling-place. This was the place where he wished to be worshipped, and where his blessing was communicated to men. This was the place of pilgrimage towards which the faith and longing of the scattered Jewish people were directed. This was the holiest spot on earth.

By the seventh century B.C. the Jerusalem Temple had quite clearly achieved this position of eminence in the religious life and thought of the chosen people. Actually, its existence as a symbol of Yahweh dwelling with and protecting his people led to a false complacency. The people considered their salvation automatic because of the Temple and its cult. Several of the great prophets, like Jeremiah, tried to awaken the populace to the superficiality of their faith and to turn them to a more genuine practice of their religion. But it took the Babylonian conquest of Jerusalem and the destruction of the Temple, in 586 B.C., to shatter the ill-founded security of the men of Jerusalem.

Taken from their homeland, dwelling as a subject people at Tel-abib on the banks of the Chebar in Babylon, without king or Temple or cult, the exiles from Jerusalem faced a severe religious crisis. Apparently, Yahweh no longer blessed the land of Israel, not even the place of his dwelling in Jerusalem's Temple. With Yahweh's presence withdrawn, Jerusalem was no longer the holy city, no longer the center of salvation. Actually, this was the way that Ezekiel, the great prophet of the exile community, saw in vision the destruction of Jerusalem: the "glory of Yahweh," i.e., the bright shining manifestation of Yahweh's saving presence, departed from the Temple and went up through the heavens, thus symbolizing Yahweh's departure from the Holy of Holies (Ezek. 11:22-23).

But in a later vision Ezekiel saw a rebuilt Temple and the return of the "glory" to its sacred precincts — a vision that was a promise to the exiles of Jerusalem's restoration as a holy city (Ezek. 40-47). Encouraged and guided by this vision, the exiles did return to rebuild the Temple, and from the time of Ezra onward the Jerusalem Temple occupied a place of privileged uniqueness in the people's life, more so than at any time before the Babylonian exile.

It is not surprising that much of the theological understanding of the Temple and its role developed in the traditions of the Temple priesthood. Immersed as they were in the service of Yahweh in the Temple, the Jerusalem priests naturally tended to interpret all of Israel's faith and traditions in the light of their own religious role. No group would be as likely to see the Temple and its sacrificial liturgy as the center of Yahweh's presence to the people, and we know from a literary analysis of the Old Testament books that this mentality actually characterized the priestly traditions.

Ezekiel, himself probably from the high-priestly family, reflects this viewpoint in his prophecies, particularly in the visions of the rebuilt Temple. He sees the Temple, not only as built again and the place of Yahweh's worship, but as the source and center of salvation and life. This vision is expressed in poetic fashion: he sees the waters of life flowing out from the Temple to the four corners of the earth (Ezek. 47).

There is a problem in evaluating this concentration of Israel's religion in Jerusalem and in its Temple worship. Can one who accepts in faith the basic reality of God's special dealings with the people of Israel see this preeminence of Jerusalem as an intrinsic element of Old Testament revelation? Is the activity of God to be tied this exclusively to one place?

The presence and role of the Temple undoubtedly did effect in the thinking and experience of the Jewish people a sacralization of the world. The Temple was the holy place and all other places were seen in relationship to it. However, when one reads the Bible and sees the century-long polemic that was undertaken by the Jerusalem priesthood to establish the claim of the Temple as the unique shrine to Yahweh, one wonders to what extent this human factor accounts for the historical preeminence of the Temple. And if the "localization" of Yahweh's saving presence was due to human interpretation, how truly compatible with God's action in history is the sacralization of space in terms of one "sacred center"?

Probably there is no possibility of sorting out the divine and human influences that shaped the faith of Israel, specifically her faith in the unique salvific role of the Jerusalem Temple. There is no doubt that the Temple played a critical and positive role in the historical development of Israel as a community of believers in Yahweh. The Temple with its priesthood and cultic liturgy was a pivotal influence in preserving, purifying, and communicating the sacred traditions that molded Israel's faith. Without the reality of the Jerusalem Temple, the Old Testament process of "salvation history" would have been utterly other than it actually was. And for one who accepts the Old Testament in faith this process somehow contains the revelation about human life that God is giving us.

On the other hand, there is the danger that the "centralizing" of God in some spot like the Jerusalem Temple will limit man's understanding of the divine. One can constantly repeat the statement that God is not confined to a given sacred place, but the very existence of such a privileged place can continue to give the impression that that is where God actually is if one is interested in contacting him.

Again, the confining of God's revealing presence to a particular place can give the custodians of that place the impression that God belongs to them. And if the place, like Jerusalem, has national as well as religious significance, there is the danger that God comes to be looked upon as a national divinity rather than as the Lord of the universe.

Looking ahead to the New Testament, one sees that this precise problem was faced by Jesus and the early Christian community, and that a fundamentally new approach was taken. One of the major themes of the Gospels is the relationship of Jesus to the Jerusalem Temple and its established priesthood. That Jesus was seen as a threat to the privileged position of the Temple worship seems clear. From an early stage in his public ministry the high priests of Jerusalem were worried about his influence and his message. Their opposition to him grew to the point where they instigated his death.

Nor was the worry of the high priests unfounded. The Gospels make it clear that Jesus was the replacement of the Temple. "Destroy this temple, and in three days I will raise it up . . . he spoke of the temple of his body" (Jn. 2:19). And the only charge made against Jesus in his trial before the Sanhedrin that is recorded in the Gospels is this very matter: "We heard him say, 'I will destroy this temple that is made with hands and in three days I will build another, not made with hands'" (Mk. 14:58).

It was in Jesus himself that God was specially present. He was the "glory" of his Father, that is the manifestation in the world of his Father's saving love. His presence as man in the world gave to the world a sacralization that it had never had up to that point. God himself, become man, was now an intrinsic part of that world. God's dwelling with men was realized, not in a city or a building, but in a man.

While this new approach to God's sanctifying presence in the world came to sharp and clear expression in Christ and early Christianity, it was not totally lacking in the Old Testament period. Besides the dwelling of Yahweh in the Temple, there was also a special presence of their God to some of the charismatic figures of Israel, especially to the prophets. The existence of a prophet in Israel was seen as a manifestation of Yahweh's continuing favor to his people, but it was not seen as something that could parallel, much less challenge, Yahweh's dwelling in the Holy City and its Temple.

The experience of living in a spatial world was made sacred for the Israelites, most basically, by the promised land. Even the role of Jerusalem and its Temple fitted into this picture. The favor that extended to the whole land found, as it were, a more concentrated expression in Jerusalem, although this was a view that was not completely accepted by those who lived in the countryside. The land of Israel was a sacred spot, the most sacred spot in the world, because Yahweh had blessed it specially and planted his own chosen people in it (Is. 35). This was the place where his name was invoked in praise and thanksgiving; this is where he received the glory that was his due.

Other places and peoples could also be blessed or cursed by Yahweh, but this happened in accord with their attitude to Israel: "I will bless those who bless you; and I will curse those who curse you." This land stood, in the Israelitic view of the created world, at the center of the universe: the other nations on all sides, the heavens above, and Sheol below. An appropriate arrangement, since their sacred traditions told them that Yahweh had promised to Abraham that ". . . by your descendants shall all the nations of the earth bless themselves" (Gen. 22:18).

But whether one considers the function of the Temple, or the kings, or the prophets, or the land itself, as "locating" Yahweh in the midst of the people and making Israel a sacred place, one is inevitably brought back to the realization that the sacralizing principle is always Yahweh. If the life experience of being in the world was distinctive for the Old Testament Israelites, this was not because the world was sacralized by the presence of divinity. The experience was distinctive precisely because the god in question was Yahweh, a god utterly different from the other gods of the ancient world.

"Demythologizing" in Israel

One of the most fascinating aspects of Old Testament thought is the way in which Israel's theologians "demythologized" other ancient explanations of the world. Situated as they were in the midst of several culturally rich ancient civilizations, the Israelites were exposed to a fairly extensive collection of religious myths — Egyptian, Babylonian, Canaanite, Persian, Greek. The biblical literature gives ample evidence that the mythic thinking of these various cultures had a broad and continuing effect on many aspects of Israel's thought and life. At the same time, no element of myth, whether it concerned "creation" or kingship or the seasons of the year, came into Israel untouched; it soon underwent a process of "demythologizing."

It was not unusual for the myths of primitive religions gradually to undergo scrutiny as cultures grew more sophisticated and self-aware. But the general pattern revealed in the history of religion is that the advance of either science or philosophy, or both, is the source of the demythologizing. As men become more aware of the physical forces at work in nature, they can now give an account of physical phenomena in these terms and no longer need to invoke stories about the gods. The more science and philosophy advance, the more the educated class abandons the ancient myths, or keeps them simply as part of a literary tradition.

Most likely there was a little of this development in Israel, but the more important challenging of the ancient myths was effected by the impact of Yahweh on the thinkers of Israel. It was the reality of Yahweh himself that made the myths unacceptable. If he was the only god, if he was the creator of the universe and of man, if he was the one who guided the course of mankind's life, then there was no place for the likes of Tiamat or Marduk or Baal. Israel did not produce scientific thinkers, so the thought of the Old Testament accepts without question the basic "cosmology" of the ancient world: a flat world, covered with a dome called the "heavens," surrounded by water, etc. But Israel did produce theologians, and these men challenged the mythic understanding of what lay at the source of the cosmos. Yahweh alone was the ultimate source and cause of the created world.

The early chapters of Genesis show clearly the poetic nature of the "theology" expressed there and its obvious relationship to the mythic literature of the ancient Near East. Perhaps no "episode" in this account of men's origins is more fancifully described than that of his short sojourn in the garden of paradise. From the point of view of the Old Testament sacralization of space, the explanation of paradise is both fascinating and very important.

For some reason that is difficult to ascertain with accuracy, the myth of a "paradise lost" is found almost universally, though it can take quite diverse forms, as in the story of Gilgamesh or that of Pandora's box. Perhaps the myth reflects a feeling that all humans have, a feeling of being alienated in the world, of never being totally at home, and expresses this feeling in the nostalgic longing for "the good old days," the golden age before everything went wrong.

Israel obviously shared in this sense of displacement, of exile from an ideal homeland, of suffering because of some primeval "fall." Yet for Israel, at least in the thought reflected in the pages of Genesis, this sense of exile was largely alleviated by her possession of the promised land. True, the land of Israel was not paradise. There were droughts, and the land gave up its fruit only by dint of hard human labor. But it was a land of wheat and grape and olive, a land that could poetically and by way of exaggeration be called "a land flowing with milk and honey." Many passages in the Old Testament suggest strongly that the conquest of the promised land was a partial regaining of paradise.

By the time that Israel's theologians explained reflectively the origins of man, the chosen people were already firmly in possession of their land, although they may have been in Babylonian exile during the final stage of this reflection. At any rate, the reality of the land of Israel was a point of reference from which they could look back to the "place" from which they originated — and paradise was the place where that long series of wanderings began that ultimately brought Yahweh's people to their own land.

Quite naturally, and with no apologies for chauvinistically centering the world's development on themselves, the Israelites looked upon the origins of mankind as the pre-history of the people of Israel. They viewed the first couple, shaped by the hand of God, as the parents of all the earth's peoples, although they also saw the line of special descent and destiny as gradually narrowing until it came to focus in the people of Israel. So, while Adam was the ancestor of the entire race, he was preeminently the ancestor of Israel. In such a mentality, it is not surprising that the people's experience of living in the land of Israel was a subtle influence on the manner in which they thought about man's first dwelling place.

Homeless wandering was an experience that was lodged deeply in the collective memory of the Israelites. Their ancestors had traveled from their ancient home in the Mesopotamian valley, and eventually found their way westward to the land of the Canaanites, probably as part of the large-scale migration of peoples in the second millenium before Christ. Most likely the life of the patriarchal period was still largely nomadic, and while the sojourn in Egypt was more stable, the tribes who dwelt there never looked upon it as a settled existence. Then followed the years of the desert wandering, and finally the entry into their own land.

But even after the Israelites secured their land from the Canaanites and the Philistines, the story was not ended; the destruction of the northern kingdom of Israel by the Assyrians and the Babylonian conquest of Jerusalem spread the tribes of Israel throughout the ancient Near East. Some few of them, largely of the tribe of Judah, came back to their own land after the Babylonian exile, but the greater portion remained scattered in the Diaspora.

It is logical, then, that Israel's traditions and reflections about the origins of man should have stressed the notion that man is an exile from paradise, destined to spend long centuries in wandering. But for the Israelites that wandering was not completely pointless; it was meant some day to terminate in the land that Yahweh would give them. As Israel looks on the tragic story of paradise lost, she sees her ancient ancestor exiled from the garden, but she also sees mankind beginning at that spot the long journey that will lead to the promised land.

If the land that the Israelites possessed (in one fashion or another) for about a thousand years had an influence on the way in which they thought about the original place of human dwelling, the idyllic garden of paradise, this same land molded their thinking about the future. The restored and triumphant people of Yahweh would dwell in a situation of prosperity in their land, and on that day the land of Israel would "become like the garden of Eden" (Ezek. 36).

The paradise overtones in Israel's expectations of the messianic era are subtle, but quite apparent. One does not find the future golden age explicitly referred to as a "return to paradise," but many of the elements associated with the biblical description of the original state of mankind are to be found in the passages that speak of the future golden age, the glorious "day of the Lord." In that future day of triumph and salvation even the deserts will flow with water, the lion and the lamb will lie down together in peace (Is. 11:6-9).

And all of this will take place in the promised land, or at least the latter will be the center of this happy situation. No longer will this sacred land be overrun and devastated by the armies of predatory empires. Yahweh will have crushed

Israel's enemies, and these enemies will come in acknowledgment of Yahweh and of Israel to seek salvation. Toward
the end of the Old Testament period there developed an
apocalyptic current of thought (to be investigated in the
next chapter) which looked for the resolution of Israel's
destiny in some extra-temporal and extra-spatial "heaven."
But such was not the viewpoint of the great prophets of
Israel, nor was it that of the unknown "theologians" who
refined and expressed in the biblical literature the faith and
traditions of the chosen people. For them the attainment of
mankind's destiny, the final "coming home" after centuries
of wandering amidst darkness and sinfulness, was tied to
this promised land that had been the goal of Israel's first
exodus.

In that glorious "day of the Lord," Jerusalem would come
definitively into its own and the Temple would be for all
men the center of worship and salvation. All nations would
have recognized Israel's history as a witness to the reality of
Yahweh and his merciful providence, and they would praise
his holy name. Jerusalem would truly be the sacred center
of the world; all nations would be blessed because of it
(Is. 62).

That this glorious future situation of Jerusalem and its
Temple was seen, at least by some of Israel's thinkers, as a
"paradise regained" is indicated by the final chapters of the
book of Ezekiel, which we mentioned earlier (Ezek. 40-47).
In vision the prophet sees the Temple rebuilt in even greater
splendor, and springing forth from it the life-giving waters
that flow to all parts of the world. This is clearly meant to
indicate that from Jerusalem Yahweh will bestow the basic
gift of salvation, life itself, on all men. And the connection
with the biblical description of man's original situation in
paradise seems evident: In the second chapter of Genesis
the river that flows through Eden to make it fruitful and
life-giving divides to form the great rivers of the world (Gen.
2-10).

We might, then, reflect briefly on Israel's view of the world and on the way in which the reality of Yahweh's saving presence (which the Israelites accepted in faith) sacralized the world. In general, they were quite optimistic about the world, surprisingly so in the light of their historical experiences of conquest and oppression. For the Israelites the world was essentially good from its very origin. As Yahweh brings the world and man into existence, he pauses at each step to notice that what he has done is good (Gen. 1). Not even the anguished questioning of Israel's "wisdom movement," reflected in the books of Ecclesiastes and Job, is able ultimately to shake this conviction that the world is good, that it is a blessing which Yahweh has bestowed on men.

For Israel the world is not only good, it is sacred because of her god Yahweh. The Israelites live surrounded by his presence, guided by his law that directs them to true wisdom, blessed by the fruitful land that he has given them as their heritage. The basic world-view of Israel is, then, grounded in faith in Yahweh, and made distinctive by that faith. The very structures of the Israelites' experience as "persons in the world" were what they were because Yahweh had revealed himself to them.

"Sacred" Institutions

However, human beings, at least as we know them from historical evidence, do not experience the phenomenon of space simply in terms of the physical universe in which they are located. They are also surrounded in their experience by the things that man has built, by the structures of society through which men have institutionalized their ideas and hopes and fears and faith. We have just seen, for example, the extent to which Israel's sacralizing of the spatial world was controlled by the reality of the Jerusalem Temple.

This raises a fundamental problem for any group of believers who hold, as both Jews and Christians do, that God somehow reveals himself to men in and through life in the world. Granting that the world of nature has a sacred character because it comes from the creator as a blessing for men, what can one say about the way in which men themselves have institutionalized their life in this world? Can one say that God sacralizes these human institutions, so they too can serve as a medium of his self-revelation? Or are not these institutions likely to develop apart from the influence of God's "word," even perhaps in opposition to that word?

Nor can religious institutions escape such questioning; as a matter of fact, they are most importantly involved in such an appraisal. If the institutionalized forms of religion do not honestly translate the faith of the religious community, the faith of this community is in danger of being perverted. Moreover, institutionalized expressions of faith that may have been adequate in one period of history may no longer be relevant in a later period when faith has grown in insight and maturity.

To put the problem in the terminology that is being widely used in theological circles today: If a community of believers (like the Jews or the Christian Church) is to safeguard the essential continuity of its faith, must it not constantly face the task of introducing a certain discontinuity (i.e., change) into its institutional life? The practical answer to this question is dangerous, unavoidably so. If too much discontinuity occurs, the believing community loses contact with its roots, with its traditions, with the faith of earlier generations, and therefore with the source of its own faith. On the other hand, if no change, no discontinuity in institutions occurs, the dynamism of the life of faith may be throttled.

While this problem is of critical importance for Christianity today because of the rapidly accelerating extent to which man-made patterns of life, such as urbanization, are shaping human experience, it is not a new problem. Ancient Israel and the primitive Christian community both had to face it. And while the experience of these two groups as it is conveyed to us in the pages of the Bible does not provide us with any ready-made solutions to our own situation, it may help to clarify the relevant questions and provide some guidelines for their answers.

Since we have already indicated the important role played by two Old Testament institutions, the kingship and the Temple, in Israel's sacralizing of space, it might be good to look again at them and question their effectiveness as expressions of Israel's faith in Yahweh. For Christians there is a special reason for examining these two patterns of Israel's life, since part of early Christianity's explanation of the role of Jesus was in relation to the Old Testament kingship and to the Temple: Jesus as Messiah is the fulfillment of the kingship, and he is also the fulfillment of the Jerusalem Temple.

The case of the Temple is particularly critical, since it became for the later centuries of the Old Testament period a primary institutionalization of Israel's faith. Moreover, it provides an excellent example of the continuity/discontinuity problem we are discussing, since it was both similar to and different from Israel's earlier cultic institutions.

There is every reason to assume that the people of Israel, from the very beginnings of their historical existence, externalized their relation to Yahweh in cultic forms. Exactly what these early cult practices were is impossible to establish by historical study, but the descriptions we have in the Pentateuch of the Tabernacle and the Ark of the Covenant seem rooted in very ancient traditions. Both the Tabernacle and the Ark functioned as sensible symbols of the presence of Yahweh to his people. The former, a tent that was pitched wherever the Israelites in their desert wandering settled down for a period, was basically an oracle-situation, a "contact point" with Yahweh to which Moses and the people could come for divine guidance (Num. 16:15-24). The Ark seems to have been viewed as a portable throne of judgment from which Yahweh exercised his power in the midst of the people and in battle (1 Sam. 4-5).

When the wandering tribes entered the promised land under Joshua and settled down in the land of Canaan, the mobility of the earlier cult was replaced by worship that took place in a number of shrines. Several of these are mentioned by name — Dan, Gilgal, Bethel, Shiloh — and it seems that some form of Yahwistic cult did occur in these shrines during the period of the tribal confederacy and for a long time thereafter. However, the traditions that passed into the book of Judges seem to indicate that the scattered situation of the people during the period of the confederacy prevented any clear definition of the cult or its confinement to the major shrines. What does seem clear is that by the end of the period of the judges, at the time of Samuel, the shrine at Shiloh had a special role because of its possession of the Ark of the Covenant.

With David's establishment of Jerusalem as his capital and his transfer of the Ark to Jerusalem, a new context for cult begins to develop. David's actions set in motion a tendency towards the centralization of Israel's worship, a tendency that was greatly intensified by the building of the Temple under Solomon. However, it would be a serious misreading of history to think that the Jerusalem Temple immediately became the exclusive place of Israel's cult. Actually, it took long centuries and a number of historical happenings — the destruction of the northern kingdom by the Assyrians, the repressive moves of Josiah against other shrines (during the late seventh-century Deuteronomic reform) and the Babylonian conquest of Jerusalem — to bring about the definitive centralization of worship in the Temple.

Centralization, though, was not the only change in Israel's cultic life that took place because of the Jerusalem Temple. The origin of this national shrine as the royal shrine, its location in the capital city of the kings of Judah, and the prominent role that the king most likely played in some of the great cultic celebrations would have opened the way for ideas connected with kingship to affect Israel's cultic attitudes and therefore its cultic forms. Yahweh was appealed to for support of the kings in their military adventures, and his relationship to the worshipping community was seen in terms of his covenant with the Davidic dynasty (e.g. Ps. 20).

Not only was Yahweh viewed in relation to the Davidic kings, as their patron and protector, but Yahweh himself tended to be seen in kingly fashion, as ruling not only men on earth but also the "heavenly court." This kingly image was applied to Yahweh in the cult of the Temple, as the Psalms attest, long after the disappearance of kingship from the social life of Israel. Probably this practice was reinforced by the way in which the high priesthood of the Temple, in the period after the restoration of the Temple, took to themselves some of the aura and trappings of the former kingship.

The evidence seems to indicate, then, that the centuries of the Old Testament saw a measurable change in the institutionalized forms of worship, mirroring a change in the understanding the people had of Yahweh. Jerusalem gradually became the only acceptable place for celebration of the great festivals; the imagery of the political state was applied to religion; and a complicated system of liturgical actions was developed by the Temple priesthood.

Yet along with this change there was a continuity with Israel's faith-traditions. Moreover, this continuity was cherished and constantly appealed to by the priestly traditions. The god who was worshipped in the Temple was unquestionably "the god who brought your fathers out of Egypt," and the covenant that was commemorated and reaffirmed in the Temple festivals was the covenant that began at Sinai. The ancient Tabernacle and Ark were seen as forerunners and protoypes of the Temple itself, and the high priesthood was traced back to Moses' appointment of his brother Aaron as priest.

Granting a basic legitimacy to this priestly claim of fidelity to Israel's traditions, one still wonders to what extent the full reality of the Temple and its liturgy can be claimed as "of divine origin." Can one, even within the context of Israel's faith, say that Yahweh intended the Temple and its cult to develop in the way it actually did? Or did not this worship, simply because it was constructed by men, derive in part from authentic insights of faith, but also in part from the theories about worship and sacrifice developed by the Temple priesthood, as well as from the contingent needs of changing historical circumstances and from the cult of other religions to which Israel was exposed? We do know, as a matter of fact, that all of these factors influenced the very way the Temple was built, and the way in which its sacrificial rituals developed.

For a man of faith in today's world, what can the Old Testament Temple and its ritual tell us about the manner in which God should be worshipped? Certainly a large part of the Temple's historical function applied only to the religious needs of the Old Testament Jews, and even if these needs were genuinely provided for at that time, we cannot conclude today that we should worship in like manner. But are there more universal elements in Israel's Temple worship that belong to what we can call "revelation"; elements that translate the deeper insights of Israel's faith and that, therefore, must find some appropriate expression in our contemporary worship?

To give just one example: we may have to pass the judgment that the Temple's claim to exclusive centralization was excessive (even for its own day) and certainly not meaningful for us today. But implicit in this claim was the notion that the Temple and its ritual were meant to form a community of believers — and is this not a perennial purpose of the worship of God?

For a Christian the ultimate answer to these questions must be given in the light of the Gospel teaching that Jesus is the replacement of Jerusalem's Temple. This is not to say that the institutions of Old Testament religion possess no intrinsic meaning of their own. Rather, it is to say that these institutional forms are part of the historical development of a people who are striving to give expression to their understanding of God; and that the criterion for judging both this understanding and its institutional translation is the understanding that Jesus had (and has) of himself and of his Father.

The Kingship

When we evaluate the religious role of Israel's kingship we encounter again a reality that is difficult to assess. But the assessment must take place, even if inadequately, by anyone who seeks a critical and mature understanding of Christianity. There is a widespread tendency among men to mix their thinking about religion and politics, to apply models of political life to the structuring of religious practice, and to consider political structures as sacred realities. Our own day is no exception in this regard. Yet it does seem that something new may be developing today in our thinking on this subject. For example, Vatican II in its Constitution on the Church describes the Church not so much in images drawn from political models (as we have done for many centuries) as in images drawn from the New Testament (body of Christ, family of God). On the other hand, our American political life is moving away from the implicitly acknowledged status of Protestantism as "the established religion" and towards the neutrality that the American Constitution espouses. In this contemporary process of reappraisal a Christian may well be aided by reflection upon the institution of kingship in Israel.

In the concrete reality of Old Testament history, the kingship, both in the northern kingdom of Israel and in the southern kingdom of Judah, unquestionably contributed to the advance of religion. Because of the national unification achieved under this political structure the people attained a unified identity such as they had not had before. Moreover, the royal court provided a center for the development of a literary culture and for the production of those literary forms (poetry, court annals, proverbs and aphorisms, songs) in which the religious traditions of the people could be expressed. More directly the kings could, and did, support financially the shrines and other religious establishments. And on occasion — as in the case of Josiah during the religious reforms of the late seventh century — the kings lent their political power to the task of establishing authentic Yahwistic religion among the people.

On the other hand, it is not always clear that the role of the king was one of support rather than of interference. Much more basically, it is not clear that most of the kings saw their role as one of serving the well-being of the people rather than exploiting the people for the achievement of dynastic goals. What many of them seemed to have aimed at was a context of life in which their subjects would see the world around them as sacralized not so much by the presence of Yahweh as by the presence of the king himself. Such a prostitution of religion to serve the purposes of the political state is equivalently idolatry, for it gives the sacralizing role of Yahweh to the king — where the king is, there is salvation.

Thus the actual role of Old Testament kingship is enigmatic. Even more so than the Jerusalem Temple, the contribution of the kingship to Israel's advance in faith was questioned even in the Old Testament period. The historical failure of the kings, including the Davidic dynasty, did much to throw doubt on the intrinsic need for kingship and on its "divine origin." However, we must not forget (at least if we wish to read the Bible honestly) that in the post-exilic period, when the Jews learned from experience that the land could be a sacred place without the presence of a king, they still kept their messianic expectancies, which were grounded ultimately in the tradition of the promise made by Yahweh to David.

Short of a careful theological analysis of Jesus' messianic role, it is impossible to give a Christian appraisal of Old

Testament kingship. Even with the New Testament teaching as a guide, specifically its teaching that Jesus, the Messiah, is the manifestation of God's presence with us, Christian thought has not been able to clarify with satisfaction the question that Old Testament kingship raises. Perhaps the most we can learn at the present is the danger inherent in linking the life of faith too closely with political institutions. In the next chapter, we will study the protest of Israel's prophets against the damaging influence of both religious and political institutions on the people's life of faith. This may throw further light on the subject.

Religion Without Institutions

History indicates that religious institutions always create a certain number of problems. They never seem to be an adequate expression of a religious community's basic faith; by definition it is impossible for them to be this. Like any externalization of man's life in society they tend to become static and "established," while life itself is more dynamic and seeks always to advance. The more detailed the institution becomes in its guidance of the community's expression of faith (as we see from the law and the liturgy in the later centuries of Old Testament history), the greater is the danger of a suffocating legalism and, correlatively, of a superficial external practice of religion.

More than once, men have reflected on these problems and drawn the conclusion that the answer lies in a religion without institutions, a religion constituted purely by the internal faith of believers. Yet this conclusion seems to be an impossible ideal, if indeed it is even an ideal. Institutions are intrinsic and necessary to human existence; men must give expression to their internal consciousness or this very consciousness becomes impossible. And these institutions, whatever they may be, form an important element in the world of space and time in which men identify and locate themselves.

Perhaps in a religious context like that of Buddhism one might see the possibility of dispensing with any strictly religious institutions (though historically Buddhism has not done this). Because there is, ultimately, a pantheistic world-view at the basis of Buddhism, it is open to a total indentification of "secular" and "sacred," with the secular institutions of human life sufficing to sacralize man's experience.

But the faith of the Old Testament people and of Christians points to something else, as we have tried to explain. This faith holds that a transcendent god, a god who stands "face to face" with the men he has created, has intervened in human experience and made that experience sacred by his special presence. The world in which men live is "sacred space" because of that special presence of God. But that world of itself does not speak this presence. Precisely because this presence (if we grant its reality) is a presence to men in faith, it can be made the sensible object of man's experience only if men themselves give some external expression of their faith. Such external expression of a community's faith is what we mean by religious institutions.

This does not mean that we settle fatalistically for the inadequacies of religious institutions. It points rather to the constant need to revise these established forms, so that they more effectively relate to and affect the changing world in which men find themselves. There is a great deal of truth in the often-quoted phrase, *ecclesia semper reformanda* ("the Church is always in need of reform"), though its practical application must always be governed by a proper balance between continuity and discontinuity.

One basic question faces a religious community if it wishes to be progressive, to move ahead with the changing patterns of man's culture, to remain relevant to man as his achievements and aspirations grow: What principle of continuity will guide the community as it modifies its external institutions, so that these modifications will not lead the community away from its original faith? To put the question in the concrete: How does the Church in the midst of the changes in its external life that circumstances seem to demand still remain the Church of Christ? How far along the road of change can the Church go before it loses its fundamental identity? And what norm can the Church use to answer this question?

Israel's experience can be instructive in this matter, for the people of the Old Testament had to wrestle with this problem on more than one occasion — each time, as a matter of fact, that the nation's sociological context underwent basic change. And one can notice that at each of these critical junctures in Israel's development there were diverse opinions on the manner in which her faith was to be preserved.

One of the recurring "solutions" proposed was that of a fundamentalist "return to the sources." According to this view the only way of safeguarding the purity of faith and tradition is to regain the simple and uncomplicated situation that existed at the origin of the religion. If only one could reestablish this original state of affairs, he could be assured that he had not abandoned the faith of his fathers.

There is an important element of validity in this view. If one is to speak seriously about religious traditions that safeguard the revelation God has given, the faith of a religious group at a later point in history must possess some ascertainable identity with the faith of the original community. If Christians, for example, are to claim today that their faith and life preserve the revelation entrusted to the first Christians, that faith and life must have elements of basic sameness with early Christianity.

But the reconstitution today of the primitive forms of Christian life is neither possible nor desirable. Even if history could be reversed, which it cannot, the external forms of an earlier period of Christian life could not speak to contemporary man the same message they spoke to Christians of that earlier age; our life experience today is not the same as theirs. Some basic core of faith and life must pass on through the centuries, otherwise there is no such thing as tradition. But to say that this must occur by a rigid retention of institutional forms is to deny to the religious community the possibility of growth and development.

As we reflect on what actually happened during the Old Testament centuries in Israel, it appears that a more fundamental principle of continuity was at work: the reality of Yahweh himself and his choice of Israel as his people. While the people's understanding of him underwent considerable change, and while a concomitant development occurred in their cultic worship and in their other social forms, Yahweh remained the same. So long as their faith remained in contact with him and their external social institutions expressed the insights of this faith, their religion possessed a radical and all-important principle of continuity. When we come to examine this principle in Christianity, as we will do later, we will discover that the faith of Christians absorbs this solution into its belief in the continuing presence of the risen Christ.

This discussion of the role played by Israel's religious institutions has really brought us back to our earlier explanation of the manner in which space was sacralized for the Old Testament Israelites. The reason why the world about them was "sacred space," in the midst of which they experienced human life, was the abiding and protecting presence of Yahweh. And to the extent that their own social institutions expressed authentically this presence of Yahweh, these institutions contributed to the process of sacralizing the world. If the faith of Israel in Yahweh's revelation of himself to her was true, we can say that God deeply affected the life of his chosen people by making their world-as-experienced a sacred context for human life.

CHAPTER THREE

A God in History

ONE OF THE most prominent elements in modern man's search
for understanding of himself and of his world is his study of
history. It is true that men for many centuries, certainly as
far back as Herodotus and Thucydides, have written historical accounts of the events of human life. Yet, it was not
until modern times that men became conscious of the extent
to which historical understanding permeates man's entire
intellectual life. Today we take it for granted that an extensive study of history is a basic element in education. School
children begin this study at an early age, and on the highest
levels of university research we find specialized aspects of
historical study as part of the various disciplines of knowledge — the history of literature, the history of science, the
history of philosophy. Our understanding of history conditions every facet of the understanding that we have of ourselves and of our world.

At the root of this historical view lies the fact that human
life and experience take place, as we discussed earlier, in the
framework of space and time. As part of the created universe our existence is sequential, that is our existing is limited
to a constantly changing "now." We actually possess only
a moving moment of existence that we call "the present";
we cannot keep the past in existence nor can we yet possess
the future. The present is always becoming the past, and
there is nothing we can do to halt this process. We are inescapably beings in time.

There is another element of human reality that makes history possible. Unlike the other beings in this world, we humans are self-aware and endowed with memory. Though the past no longer is, we can recall it and recognize it as part of the process that led up to the present. Though the existential reality of time is that of a moving point, we can, through memory, see the line that the moving point creates — a line of past, present, and future. On this continuum of time created by our conscious recall, we situate our experience of the present moment. The present is experienced as related to both past and future.

When we talk about history, however, we mean more than the fact that men are aware of existing prior to the present moment. History means that man discovers some pattern in that previous sequence, and the historical studies that characterize the intellectual endeavor of modern man are efforts to clarify that pattern. Is there really order and intelligibility in the past? Is mankind's progression through time a regularly unfolding and meaningful process? Or is it a hopelessly irrational meandering, "a tale told by an idiot"?

While the temptation to abandon the search for meaning, to view human life as essentially unintelligible, is a recurrent one, men have never been able to succumb to it. Time is too inescapably a part of our experience as spirits-in-the-world. Each of the world-views that men have had as a basis for their culture has been controlled by some image of the time sequence.

Israel and Linear Time

In general, though this generalization needs careful modification when applied to a specific cultural situation, man's image of time has been either "cyclic" or "linear." Time is an endlessly recurring pattern, a circular process without real advance; what is, already was and will be again. Or, time forms a line that is advancing into the unknown; the present is at least partially unlike the past, and the future will be some new reality with elements unlike either past or present.

In what we consider Western culture, and more specifically in what we call "modern thought," the linear image of time has been dominant. One clear instance of this dominance is the pervasive presence today of the notion of evolution. The idea of a developing process, applied not only to the biological evolution of species but to many other factors in the time sequence, is fundamentally incompatible with a cyclic image of time.

Modern scholarship has established that the origin of this linear view of time and history is to be found principally in the thought of ancient Israel. It is in the pages of the Old Testament that one finds a clear statement of mankind's odyssey in time as a purposeful journey towards a goal. Israel's theologians see human life as "eschatological" — both past and present find their meaning as part of a patterned progression toward an ultimate fulfillment of human history. The thought of Israel has, at least in this one respect, made a major contribution to our present view of the world. And if, as we will try to point out, this eschatological character of Old Testament thought is the result of Yahweh's influence on Israel's faith, the revelation of the Old Testament has deeply modified the experience we have today of human life.

Any study of eschatology in the Old Testament must focus on the great charismatic prophets of Israel. It was they, more than the members of any other group, who clarified this way of viewing human history. Faced as they were with some of the most critical moments in the life of the chosen people, they were forced to puzzle through the enigma of the apparent failure of Yahweh's election of this people and so come to a deepened understanding of the forces that shaped Israel's history.

It would be erroneous to conclude that this linear view of time and history was the invention or even the original insight of the prophets. Though they may not delineate the view as clearly and sharply as do the prophets, the earlier traditions of Israel already give expression to this progressive notion of history. The very events that are looked upon as formative of Israel — the exodus, the covenant at Sinai, the establishment of the Davidic kingship — contain in themselves the elements of expectation and promise, and therefore look ahead to future fulfillment.

When the wandering tribes free themselves from Egyptian servitude and begin their journey through the desert, it is with a definite purpose. They are on their way to the land of Canaan. What makes it possible for them to have this direction to their wandering is the guidance of Yahweh; it was he who had freed them from their Egyptian masters, it is he who has promised to them the land of Canaan, and it is he who guides their path through the desert. The enactment of the covenant at Sinai gives purpose to their exodus from Egypt, but the covenant itself is only the beginning of a new life that is meant to be realized in the land that Yahweh will give them.

Entry into the land does not bring with it full realization of their expectations. It only holds out a promise of the longed-for goal: possession of this land as their own. So, the decades of the tribal confederacy are lived with a view to the future, to the day when Yahweh will fulfill his covenant pledge to his people. *Promise* and *fulfillment* become increasingly the pattern of their understanding of their history, an implicitly eschatological view that has meaning only because of their faith in Yahweh's fidelity. Yahweh's revelation to them stands, then, at the root of their view of history.

The very manner in which the Israelites preserved, developed, and transmitted their traditions is an indication of the linear understanding of history to which we have been referring. First of all, it is noteworthy that what they handed down from generation to generation was the recollection of the "great deeds" that Yahweh had performed on their behalf. And to each new generation these traditions were given as a means by which the people could interpret the situation in which they were located. Their present was made intelligible in terms of what had been their past. What Yahweh had begun earlier for his people he was still continuing to do.

Probably the cultic celebrations, particularly in the more important shrines, played a key role in this process of handing on the traditions. Gathered together on a festive occasion, the people would, logically, have celebrated the memory of the things their covenant god had done in days past; they would have had the meaning of these things explained to them in relationship to their own needs; and they would have been challenged to accept in faith this same god, Yahweh, as their god. We do know, from the texts in the Bible, that the great feasts celebrated in the Jerusalem Temple had this character of historical recollection (Deut. 16), and there is good evidence that the same was true of Israel's cult long before the building of the Temple.

We must not think, however, that these recollections of the past were handed down in static and fossilized form. Precisely because the traditions of the past were constantly utilized to interpret the present, these traditions were reinterpreted in terms of that present. One of the most fascinating aspects of textual study of the Old Testament is the discovery of the manner in which Israel's traditions developed organically, preserving continuity with the past at the same time as they absorbed new elements from Israel's constantly changing history.

One of the most common ways in which this continuity of tradition was maintained was the "legitimation" of new experiences, or new institutions, or new understandings, by linking them with already existent factors in Israel's life. This may seem to us artificial at times as when all the wisdom developments are linked with Solomon, but it bears witness to the historical viewpoint of Old Testament thought. All that came into the unfolding experience of the chosen people

must somehow fit into a pattern, because Yahweh was directing all of it for their benefit. Therefore, no matter how
discontinuous some new element might seem to be, there
must be some intrinsic link that bound it to Yahweh's previous salvific deeds.

The Development of the Law

Israel's development of a body of law is one of the most
striking and important illustrations of this "legitimation."
In the Bible as we possess it, there is a large and complex
body of legislation that is presented as coming from Moses.
Quite obviously this attribution to Moses is not to be understood as an actual historical reality, since much of the legislation reflects a social situation centuries later than Moses'
time. Why, then, credit it to Moses?

At the origin of Israel's existence as a people there was,
very likely, little legislation that was properly their own,
perhaps only some few prescriptions relating to the worship
of Yahweh. This legislation was viewed as coming directly
from Yahweh himself; it was the expression of his will, given
to his people through the mediation of Moses. Thus, the
very notion of law in Israel was marked by the people's
faith in Yahweh. Law was the directions for life he had given
them through his servant Moses.

Inevitably, as Israel's social existence grew more complex,
there was a need for greatly expanded legislation. Much of
the detailed cultic law in a book like Leviticus reflects the
liturgical practices that grew up over the centuries, particularly in the Jerusalem Temple. Much of the rest of the law,
dealing with the various contingencies of human social conflict, was borrowed from the legal codes of other ancient
peoples and adjusted to Israel's specific needs. It seems that
as this additional legislation entered Israel's life it was as-
similated to the basic concept of the law as an expression
of Yahweh's will. The technique used to achieve this assimi-
lation was to attribute all such law to Moses. Having been

legitimized by Moses' name, the new law was incorporated into the traditions of Israel and passed on to future generations as a guide for life.

There is one point in the history of the southern kingdom of Judah at which we can see clearly this process of attributing law to Moses. Shortly after the middle of the seventh century B.C., a youthful king, Josiah, succeeded to the throne of David. He did so with the strong support of the Temple priesthood, which apparently was interested in reversing the disastrous policies that had been initiated by Manasseh earlier in the century. In any event, Josiah, in alliance with the priests, undertook a serious reform of Jewish life.

This reform movement received a strong impetus about 623, when, according to the account preserved in 2 Kings 22, a new stage of the reform was linked with the discovery in the Temple of "the book of the Law." The Temple was in the process of restoration after its earlier neglect, and it is just possible that the book of law mentioned in the text was actually discovered during the work of restoration. More likely, however, it was a code of law that was in the possession of the priesthood and that was now opportunely "found" by the high priest, Hilkiah, and brought to King Josiah.

Very likely the "book of the Law" in question is the nucleus of the biblical book of Deuteronomy. It contained elements of law derived from Israel's older traditions, but it also contained much that was later. Yet the entirety was used as covenant law, that is, as deriving from the Mosaic covenant, in the solemn ceremony of covenant renewal described in 2 Kings 23.

Almost immediately other pieces of legislation were joined to this book of the law to form the book of Deuteronomy. One can see the process of Mosaic attribution from the structure of this book, in which Moses himself is described as promulgating this entire body of law to the Israelites of exodus times. Old and new are woven together to form the latest stage in Israel's traditions about the law that Yahweh himself was giving them.

Far-reaching though it was, the Deuteronomic reform (called such because of its relationship to the Deuteronomic law) undertaken by Josiah was somewhat superficial in its effectiveness. The two great prophets of that period, Jeremiah and Zephaniah, both indicate this, and the superficiality became quite evident when the reform collapsed with the tragic death of Josiah at the battle of Megiddo in 609. This failure would seem to reflect the fact that the reform measures of Josiah and the legislation that expressed them were less than wholeheartedly approved by a large segment of the people. Here may well have been another reason for placing the reform law under the aegis of Moses. Whether such motivation was at work or not, we have a clear instance in the Deuteronomic reform of the phenomenon we noted above: There is no promulgation of royal law as such; instead the king is seen as the agent who proclaims and enforces the law of Yahweh himself.

The Priesthood and the Wisdom Movement

Two other examples may serve to illustrate the manner in which new developments were brought into conjunction with Israel's traditions and so legitimized: the Jewish high priesthood and the wisdom movement. The first of these grew, for the most part, out of structures already present in Israel; the second found much of its origin in the culture of other peoples and was brought into Israel's thought from "outside."

There were several stages in the process by which the Jerusalem Temple priesthood "proved" its claim to preside in unique fashion over the cult of Yahweh. First of all, in the early period of the Temple's existence, it was necessary to establish some basis for the eminence of this one shrine. After all, the Temple did not pre-date Solomon, and by that time many other shrines, like Gilgal or Bethel, had long-standing recognition as Yahwistic cult centers. Recognizing

the earlier validity of these shrines, the priesthood of Jerusalem, basing its position on the traditions of Yahweh's special
election of David and Solomon, looks on itself as the only
legitimate successor to the pre-Davidic situation. Once the
Temple is built in Jerusalem, it is meant to replace all the
earlier inadequate places of worship.

But the Jerusalem priesthood does not ground its existence in the Davidic traditions alone. It preserved and developed its own form of the ancient Mosaic traditions, and this
later passed into the books of the Pentateuch, particularly
into the books of Numbers and Leviticus. As one studies
these books he can see how the "new" developments associated with the Jerusalem Temple are presented as being in
continuity with Israel's earliest worship. The Temple itself
is related to the ancient Tabernacle, a link that was made
easier by the presence of the Ark of the Covenant in the
Temple, and the sacrificial cult of the Temple is retrojected
into the description of early Israel's worship of Yahweh
(cf. Lev. 14).

Secondly, there was the need, once the basic claim of the
Jerusalem priesthood had been accepted, for this group of
priests to justify its legitimacy as the official priesthood.
This need appears to have been particularly important when
the Jews returned from Babylonian captivity to rebuild the
Temple and reestablish its cult — and the issue was more
acute when it touched the office of high priest. The solution
to the problem is reflected in the genealogies that are preserved in the books of the Bible. By tracing his descent to
Sadoq — the high priest appointed by Solomon himself when
the Temple was built — a later high priest could situate himself within the sacred traditions of his people (Ezra 7:2).
Moreover, the office of high priest was traced back to Aaron,
thus linking it with the Mosaic dispensation (Ezra 7:5).

Through this process, the cultic experience of the Jews
when they worshipped in the Jerusalem Temple was brought
into the historical perspective that characterizes their reli-

gious life. What they were doing under the direction of the Temple priesthood was guaranteed as authentic worship of Yahweh. The covenant they were celebrating stood in continuity with Yahweh's action at Sinai; they were heirs to the blessings promised in that covenant.

When we examine the case of Israel's wisdom movement, the situation is somewhat different, because, as we mentioned, the current of thought referred to as "the wisdom movement" found its origins outside Israel. There are some traces of this wisdom mentality very early in the traditions of Israel, perhaps through borrowings from Egyptian and Canaanite sources. Apparently Solomon was looked upon as a striking example of the wise man, whether this reputation was grounded in the fact that he actually did compose some of the proverbs and aphorisms that characterize the early stages of wisdom literature, or in his ability to solve some of the practical riddles of life (1 Kings 3). But the flowering of the wisdom movement came around the year 500 B.C. and thereafter.

In general the wisdom literature reflects the same questioning that was going on in other ancient cultures about that same time: What sense did life make? Who really was wise, or was it even possible for men to be wise? Wasn't life just a fatalistic farce in which man was an unwitting pawn of cosmic forces? When one reads the earlier expressions of Israel's wisdom movement one feels an atmosphere somewhat foreign to the Old Testament. It is true that the questions asked and the solutions suggested are already changed by Israel's faith in Yahweh. In the book of Job, for example, the problem of cosmic justice is placed in the context of the justice of Yahweh's dealings with men. But the view of Yahweh seems more influenced by philosophical reflection than by Israel's traditional "salvation history" understanding of Yahweh.

Increasingly, however, the more traditional viewpoint asserts itself. By the time of the book of Sirach (in the second century B.C.) the notion of wisdom is thoroughly reinte-grated into Israel's characteristic frame of thought. Wisdom is to be found only in Yahweh, but Yahweh has communi-cated this wisdom to men in the law that he has given to Israel. And the great paragons of wisdom are precisely those outstanding figures of Israel's history who have observed the law with notable fidelity (Sir. 44-50).

Wisdom literature could not, however, lay claim to being part of Israel's heritage unless it was somehow seen to be rooted in Israel's own past. This is achieved, at least par-tially, by relating wisdom writing to Solomon as idealized into the great wise man. Thus legitimized, the wisdom litera-ture can be integrated into the overall view of Yahweh's providential dealings with his people, and so can function as the "word of God."

Typology and Secularization

It seems evident that the men who produced the Old Testament literature were aware of this interrelationship of elements in Israel's history, in which later and newer oc-currences were the outgrowth and fuller realization of what had preceded them. This was not a matter of inventing these relationships, but of discovering that some such link actually bound these past and present occurrences into a coherent pattern. We have become accustomed to refer to this linking of events together as "typology" and we are becoming in-creasingly aware of its importance in biblical thought.

Typology can deal with persons, or events, or institutions that are linked together in a chronological series. What links them is some significance or function that is present in all the members of the series, though the significance or func-tion is expressed differently by each member (because the historical situation is different in each case). In general, there is progression in the series, though often the man who is the first in the series (like Moses among lawgivers, or

David among kings, or Solomon among wise men) has an unparalleled eminence.

To give some examples: The event of exodus and Sinai is linked with the prophetic vocation of Elijah and with the return from Babylonian exile (and eventually, of course, with the death and resurrection of Jesus). We can see this link from the way in which both the journey of Elijah and the journey of the Babylonian exiles back to Jerusalem are described as a new exodus (1 Kings 19:4-14; Is. 49:8-13). And when we examine these related events, we can see that the biblical writers did not link them simply as a literary device. The same fundamental meaning finds expression in each of them: liberation from evil, the need to set out on a new course of life, covenant election by Yahweh. Because each of these events does manifest the same fundamental pattern, the "revelation" communicated through each of them is radically the same. Recurrently, though in developing fashion, the historical experiences of Israel are speaking the same "message": Yahweh is a saving god.

Probably the most important example of typology as applied to persons is the series of kings who are linked with messianic hope: Hezekiah, Josiah, Zerubbabel (who, though not strictly a king, was of the Davidic line). Each of them is described as a new David, as performing fairly adequately the function within Israel's life to which Yahweh had called David (2 Kings 18:22-23; Hag. 2). It is not just the obvious fact that they are descended from David, but each of them as "a good king" is a sign of Yahweh's own guidance of Israel; each of them bears the same message to the faith of the people. The significance of David for Israel's history finds expression in each of these later personages.

Typology applies not just to events and persons, but also to the institutions of Israel's social existence. The ancient Tabernacle which, at least according to Israel's traditions, was already a primitive shrine for the Israelites in their exodus wandering, is seen by later Jewish thought as a type of the Jerusalem Temple. Though the Temple was a more grandiose structure and its liturgy more impressive, it had essentially the same significance for the faith of Israel: the symbol of Yahweh's presence to his people.

Underneath this typology lies the mentality that sees in the chronological sequence of Israel's existence a pattern, a continuous process that has some unified meaning — a meaning that is being gradually unfolded in the course of Israel's history. Israel's faith grounds this intrinsic unity of the historical process in Yahweh's guidance of human life, especially of Israel's life.

There are obvious elements of discontinuity in Israel's history, some of them severe. The exodus breaks the pattern of life in Egypt; the entry into the promised land is a radical change from the years of desert wandering; the establishment of kingship represents a new approach to Israel's integrated social existence, and this pattern in turn is disrupted by the successive destructions of the two kingdoms. Yet the traditions of Israel see all of this as somehow fitting together into an intelligible pattern, as being a continuous development of Israel's life.

The moments of special discontinuity are, nevertheless, moments of peril for Israel's traditional faith. Many of the new forces or institutions that enter Israel's life — the kingship is a prominent example — seem themselves to give promise of salvation, to solve Israel's needs and problems. Using the word "secular" loosely, we might say that these new developments tend to lead the people towards a secular explanation of their situation instead of to the traditional view that their destiny depended upon the favor and power of Yahweh.

In the earlier days of her existence as a people, Israel lacked the effective agencies of national power by which she might have hoped to gain a position of security and eminence among other nations. Up to the time of David, the very existence of the tribes that made up the covenant confederacy was in constant danger. In these circumstances it is understandable that the ordinary bases for a people's social confidence — economic, military, diplomatic, cultural bases — did not figure largely in Israel's expectations for the future.

With the kingship, the situation began to change. In the southern kingdom of Judah and even more so in the kingdom of Israel to the north the kings did effect an economic betterment, and at times they possessed fairly important military resources. Living in this new and promising national context, the people of the two kingdoms naturally looked to these new social forces to achieve hopes for peace and prosperity.

The shift towards a "secular" explanation of their life was both a danger and a progression in the thought of the people. It was progression insofar as they now began to see the influence of Yahweh as working through the ordinary dynamics of human social existence, instead of intervening by extraordinary acts in man's life. This positive growth of understanding, to the degree it was a growth in faith, demanded the religious legitimation of the new social structures. The kings, for example, had to be seen as functioning on Yahweh's behalf and therefore supported by him. At least on the surface this was done. The kings claimed to be Yahweh's anointed; they claimed his favor and backing; and they claimed to be acting within the framework of Israel's traditional faith and life (2 Kings 20).

Still, the danger of losing a Yahwistic view of history was real. Unduly impressed by their own power and wisdom, and somewhat naively trustful of the effectiveness of the social institutions they themselves had created, the leaders of the people tended to appraise the present and plan for the future in terms of these secular sources of power, even exclusively in terms of them. Indications are that, for the most part, the rulers of Israel and Judah lost sight of Yahweh as the key to Israel's future.

Though the judgments passed upon the various kings by the Deuteronomic history (Judges through Kings) must be read critically, the danger of losing Israel's traditional faith was apparently greater in the northern kingdom. This may very well have been due to the relatively greater prosperity enjoyed by the north. Under Omri, in particular, the economic life of the northern kingdom flourished, largely through his shrewd alliances with commercial powers like the cities of Tyre and Sidon. He cemented his relationships with these rich and powerful Phoenician cities by the marriage of his son Ahab to the Tyrian princess Jezebel. Safeguarding his commercial interests, he simultaneously endangered the religious life of his people, for Jezebel brought with her the religious beliefs and cult of Phoenicia, and Baal entered into open competition with Yahweh for the worship of the Israelites (1 Kings 16:28-33).

Charismatic Prophecy

At this critical juncture a new and powerful movement, *charismatic prophecy,* enters the life of Israel in the person of Elijah. He was not the first prophet in the people's history. Prophets had formed a somewhat recognized group, functioning around court and shrine, for many decades; some of them had probably been quite influential, as was Nathan at David's Court. But Elijah was a new kind of prophet, a man singled out by Yahweh — as the traditions contained in the first book of Kings tell us (1 Kings 17-21) — to carry Yahweh's own word to the people.

The prophetic activity of Elijah is somewhat dramatically described in the traditions, but the essence of his prophetic function is plain. Faced with a situation in which the people were understanding their present circumstances as totally dependent on the secular power of the king or even on the false gods of Phoenicia, Elijah recalls them to their ancient traditions. Not Baal but Yahweh, the god who brought your fathers out of Egypt, is the source of Israel's blessings and the hope of the future. Only if the people abandon their worship of the false gods and convert to Yahweh, their own covenant god, can they avoid destruction (1 Kings 18).

About a century later, Amos, the first of the literary prophets, appeared on the scene to continue Elijah's message. Again it was in the northern kingdom, this time during the apparently prosperous reign of Jereboam II. And this time the charismatic nature of the prophecy was even more apparent. Amos assures us that he was not of the established prophetic circles; he was not even from the northern kingdom, but had been summoned by Yahweh to bring his word to the king and people of the north (Amos 7:14).

The "word of god" contained in the prophetic oracles of Amos was not a pleasant word, and the prophet was less than welcome as he proclaimed it. Israel and her king had abandoned their Yahwistic traditions both cultically and socially. In her cult Israel had drifted towards an idolatrous worship of false gods and an empty and formalistic worship of Yahweh; in her social life the poor and oppressed, whose dignity and rights should have been safeguarded by the covenant law, were exploited and downtrodden. Such infidelity to Israel's sacred covenant with Yahweh could not go unpunished. The northern kingdom, despite its strength, had to come to utter destruction:

> Thus says the Lord:
> "For three transgressions of Israel
>   and for four, I will not revoke the punishments;
> because they sell the righteous for silver,
>   and the needy for a pair of shoes —
> they that trample the head of the poor into the dust of the earth,
>   and turn aside the way of the afflicted;
> a man and his father go in to the same maiden,
>   so that my holy name is profaned;
> they lay themselves down beside every altar
>   upon garments taken in pledge;
> and in the house of their God they drink
>   the wine of those who have been fined."
>
> Amos 2:6-8

Israel and her king looked forward to a "day of the Lord" when they would prosper even more. Israel's hopes, Amos tells them, are vain, for the "day of the Lord" would be one of punishment. Before that punishment came in the Assyrian destruction of Samaria (the capital of the northern kingdom) in 722, another great prophet, Hosea, arose to warn the people. Describing the covenant between Yahweh and the people through the imagery of husband and wife, Hosea reminds his hearers of their traditions, of the origins of Israel when Yahweh espoused the people to himself. But now, says Hosea, Yahweh has decided to repudiate his unfaithful wife. He is giving Israel a bill of divorce; Israel is no longer his people, his chosen one (Hos. 2:2).

The charges made by Hosea against Israel and her leaders are basically the same as that contained in Amos' prophetic oracles: oppression and exploitation of the weak rather than social justice; and adulterous abandonment of Yahweh in favor of the false gods. Like Amos before him, Hosea tells the people that such infidelity cannot go unpunished by a righteous god. Israel and her superficial prosperity will be destroyed.

But for Hosea this is not the whole message. In the beautiful second chapter of the book of Hosea — the passage that introduces the husband-wife image into prophetic thought about Yahweh and Israel, thus reinterpreting both the covenant and the human institution of marriage — there are two moments in "the day of the Lord." Israel must be punished for her adultery; Yahweh will not be mocked. Yet, in spite of Israel's infidelity in prostituting herself to the false gods, Yahweh will remain faithful to his covenant promises. He will seek out fallen Israel; he will buy her back. He will woo her and win her heart, as he had done long ago when he brought her out of Egyptian servitude:

> "Therefore, behold, I will allure her,
>   and bring her into the wilderness,
>   and speak tenderly to her.

> And there I will give her her vineyards,
>   and make the Valley of Achor a door of hope.
> And there she shall answer as in the days of her youth,
>   as at the time when she came out of the land of Egypt.
> "And in that day, says the Lord, you will call me, 'My husband,'
> and no longer will you call me 'My Baal.' For I will remove
> the names of the Baals from her mouth, and they shall be
> mentioned by name no more. And I will make for you a cov-
> enant on that day with the beasts of the field, the birds of the
> air, and the creeping things of the ground; and I will abolish
> the bow, the sword, and war from the land; and I will make
> you lie down in safety. And I will betroth you to me for ever;
> I will betroth you to me in righteousness and in justice, in
> steadfast love, and in mercy. I will betroth you to me in faith-
> fulness; and you shall know the Lord."

The second moment of "the day of the Lord" will be one
of conversion and restoration. Thus, the "word of the Lord"
that Hosea conveys to his hearers is not just one of threat;
it is also a call to conversion.

For the northern kingdom of Israel neither the conversion
to Yahweh nor the restoration became a reality. Joining in
disastrous alliance with Syria against the rising power of
the Assyrian empire, Israel was thoroughly defeated, her
capital destroyed, and her people carried off into an exile
from which they never returned. But Hosea's message of
Yahweh's covenant fidelity passed to the southern kingdom
of Judah, there to influence the prophets and theologians
whose own message would help "the faithful remnant" who,
after Judah's own destruction, would return from Babylonian exile to rebuild Jerusalem.

While Amos and Hosea were preaching in the north, the
kingdom of Judah in the south was itself being challenged
by a series of charismatic prophets. One of the earliest and
greatest of these was Isaiah, whose prophetic career extends
throughout almost the entire period of Assyrian dominance.
At the time of the northern kingdom's peril, just prior to
its destruction in 722, Isaiah strives somewhat unsuccess-
fully to keep Judah's king, Ahaz, from committing himself

to a compromising political alliance. In subsequent years he acts as goad and guide for Hezekiah, the heir of Ahaz. And his prophetic career may have extended into the religiously disastrous reign of Manasseh.

Throughout his long and relatively successful prophetic career, Isaiah preached essentially the same "word of Yahweh" that his northern counterparts, Amos and Hosea, did. Recalling Judah's leaders and people to their historical traditions, Isaiah upbraids them for their infidelity to Yahweh and promises both punishment and restoration. There is, however, one important difference. In the northern prophets it was the Sinai covenant that was appealed to almost exclusively; in Isaiah the emphasis is on the Davidic covenant — on the promises made to David and on the hope of their fulfillment in and through the Davidic dynasty.

Promise and fulfillment was, of course, well established as a pattern of Israelitic thought long before Isaiah. Perhaps by the time of Solomon, the traditions of Israel were consciously arranged on the basis of this pattern: the promises made to the patriarchs, the covenant promise of the land, the entry into the land itself as a promise of future possession. We can see here the same basic eschatology noted earlier. The very notion of a promise made by Yahweh involves the mentality which looks to the future for fulfillment; the future exists to achieve for Israel the blessings that Yahweh has promised.

Though the promises of the Sinaitic covenant gradually assume greater importance for the prophets of Judah, in the early stages of southern prophetism it is the promise made to David (2 Sam. 7) that is paramount. It is on the basis of this promise that Isaiah pronounced those oracles that we have come to call "messianic," stating the expectation of a future state of justice and peace brought about by a scion of David (Is. 9:1-7).

Because of this radical link with the historical reality of the Davidic dynasty, the eschatological viewpoint of early

Judaic prophecy — and for that matter of all the great prophets — is firmly tied to an earthly achievement of Israel's destiny. Enigmatic though it be, the course of events will lead to the time when a new David will establish in the promised land a reign of justice and peace (Is. 11).

For a brief period in the latter half of the seventh century it seemed that Judah might have that king, that new David, in the person of Josiah (2 Kings 22-23). Not only did he succeed in restoring the fortunes of Judah, but he was active in purifying the religious life of his people. But the hopes were ill-founded: with Josiah's death in 609, his reform collapsed, and his successors, Jehoiachim and Zedekiah, quickly led the kingdom to its destruction by the Babylonians.

Events moved rapidly and dramatically in the two decades between Josiah's death and Jerusalem's destruction in 586. Yet the tragic reversals of those years should not have come as complete surprises to the residents of Jerusalem. Two great prophets of that period, Zephaniah and Jeremiah, had forecast just such an outcome. Jeremiah, while he had high regard for Josiah himself, had been less than impressed by the cynical superficiality with which many of the people had accepted Josiah's reform measures, and under Josiah's successors Jeremiah's career becomes one of bitter denunciation of Judah's infidelity. All elements of Judaic life, particularly Jerusalem's established leadership of priests, kings, wise men, and prophets receive his scathing judgment.

In a sense, Jeremiah proclaims the same "word of God" that had marked the previous prophets, but with him the question about the relation between Israel and Yahweh is deepened. Along with the Deuteronomic theologians, to whom he seems closely related, he asks whether the covenant is absolute and irrevocable or whether it may not cease to be because of Israel's continued infidelity. His oracles of restoration and fulfillment, even of messianic fulfillment, indicate that he saw the covenant promises as ultimately absolute.

Nevertheless, Jeremiah raises a second aspect of this same question: granted that Yahweh's faithful mercy will ultimately triumph over the stubborn infidelity of the people, will this fulfillment take place through the institutional forms — law, temple, king — that Israel had known up to this point? To this question the book of Jeremiah gives an answer that is far from clear. There is the critical text in Jeremiah 31:31 which speaks of the new covenant that Yahweh will make, "not like the covenant of old when I brought your fathers out of the land of Egypt":

> Behold, the days are coming, says the Lord, when I will make a new covenant with the house of Israel and the house of Judah, not like the covenant which I made with their fathers when I took them by the hand to bring them out of the land of Egypt, my covenant which they broke, though I was their husband, says the Lord. But this is the covenant which I will make with the house of Israel after those days, says the Lord: I will put my law within them, and I will write it upon their hearts; and I will be their God, and they shall be my people. And no longer shall each man teach his neighbor and each his brother, saying, "know the Lord," for they shall all know me, from the least of them to the greatest, says the Lord; for I will forgive their iniquity and I will remember their sin no more.

This oracle certainly seems to look forward to some new level of Yahweh's dealings with Israel, to a situation when the faith of the people will be more interiorized, to an activity of Yahweh on people's lives and faith that will be more direct. But even this new covenant will stand in continuity with Yahweh's age-old election of Israel, for the text ends with the classic Sinaitic formulation: "I will be your god; and you will be my people." Whatever this new covenant is to be, it will stand in continuity with Israel's traditions and be made intelligible through those traditions.

With Jeremiah, then, we find the problem of continuity and discontinuity presented in increased depth. Perhaps most, if not all, of the forms through which Israel had given expression to its faith would have to disappear, for they had proved themselves inadequate. But if they did disappear, what would provide the continuity for Israel's history, what would safeguard the faith of the people and the word of salvation that Yahweh had entrusted to them?

Exile and Return

Hated though he was because of his biting criticism of the established officialdom of his day, Jeremiah was a providential preparation for the crisis of exile. The questions he had raised with prophetic vision before Jerusalem's downfall now became unavoidable for the Jews in Babylonian exile. Without king or Temple or cult or social structure of their own, all sensible links with the past were gone, and they could well ask themselves if the covenant under which they had previously lived had come to an end. To all appearances Yahweh no longer protected and guided them. There were no signs now of his blessing them as his chosen people.

Only one choice was left to the deportees from Jerusalem, if, as at least some of them did, they wished to retain their faith and their identity as Yahweh's people. They could cling in faith to Yahweh's fidelity to his promises. That many of them did so is due in large part to the fact that Yahweh still spoke to them through the prophetic voice, especially through Ezekiel, who was the first charismatic prophet to receive his call outside the promised land (Ezek. 1:1-3).

Like Isaiah and Amos and Jeremiah before him, Ezekiel accused the people of their abandonment of Yahweh, and urged them to radical conversion. The bitter fruit of exile was the logical result of the fact that Israel had become a false vine, betraying the god who had planted it with such care in the promised land. Though she had the terrifying example of her wicked sister-kingdom Israel to warn her, the kingdom of Judah had not learned the lesson and had herself gone into adulterous worship of false gods (Ezek. 16). The shepherds of Israel, the leaders of the people, had not cared for the poor and weak but had consumed them in quest of wealth and power (Ezek. 34).

So, the exiles dwell once more in an alien land, settled disconsolately on the banks of the Chebar near Babylon. But Yahweh will not leave them there; he himself will be their shepherd and lead them back to his own pasturage (Ezek. 34:11-16). The dead bones of Israel will once more rise by the power of his spirit, and Israel will live (Ezek. 37:1-14). Even Jerusalem will be rebuilt and the Temple arise in renewed splendor. For Yahweh is ever mindful of his promises.

Israel's history had not, then, come to an end. Rather, the exile was an interlude during which Yahweh would still watch over his people, and after which he would lead them back to the promised land, there to resume — now with converted hearts and minds — the task he had given them. In exile, when external religious institutions could not serve as principles of continuity, it was Yahweh himself and his word in the mouth of the prophet that preserved the continuing pattern of Israel's existence.

From another point of view, the Babylonian exile was not at all an interlude in history. Israel's history is, most importantly, the history of its development in faith, and therefore of its witness to the word of God. Even for one who is not himself a believer in Judaism or in Christianity, it is the religious development of Israel that is most distinctive of that people and therefore of most interest to the student of ancient cultures. If one is a believer, the growth of faith in ancient Israel is of major interest, for in that history of faith one can see reflected the divine action on Israel. And from this perspective the bitter experience of Babylonian exile was not a setback in Israel's development, but (at least for a select group) a moment of reflection, discovery, and conversion.

Faith did continue and even flourish in the exile community. It was precisely during these years that much of the gathering together of Israel's traditions took place. There had, of course, been many centuries of safeguarding and transmitting the sacred traditions of the people, but it seems that the final stage in the synthesis and editing of large sections of the Bible occurred in the Babylonian exile. The Pentateuch, the "Deuteronomic history," a large section of the Psalter, several of the prophetic books — all of these were in existence and utilized as a collection of sacred writings by the end of the exile.

Leaving aside the difficult technical questions about the manner in which this canon of biblical writings came into being, we can reflect on the mentality that must have been present in the Babylonian exiles as they participated in this process. Obviously they had not abandoned their ancient faith. Had they done so, they would not have bothered to preserve the record of that faith. On the contrary, in the midst of the apparently meaningless situation in which they found themselves in Babylon they searched for some meaning by pondering their past. Without anything in their captivity that promised hope for their future as a people, they could find a basis for hope only in Yahweh's earlier election of Israel.

The force of circumstances drove the Babylonian exiles back to their traditions. Only in clinging to these could they find grounds for their own social identity. If Yahweh had chosen their ancestors and formed them into his chosen people, as their traditions said; if he had pledged himself to this people in undying fidelity, which the traditions also said; if he had promised to punish Israel, but then to restore her, as the prophetic traditions in particular proclaimed; then the Babylonian exiles could still believe that they were the chosen people, that even their disastrous present had some ultimate meaning, and that they would at some future time be restored to prosperity in their own land.

The exiled Jews were forced back to Yahweh as the only principle of intelligibility for their history. In fact, the exile helped to dispel some of the excessive secularizing of their historical outlook that had crept in earlier. Without any of the secular forces — dynastic, economic, military — that could promise them hope for a future of their own, the exiles were not inclined to see such forces as the key to their existence. Instead, it was Yahweh's fidelity to his promises to which they clung. The years of exile were, then, a prime occasion for sacralizing Israel's consciousness of time.

Although the experience of Babylonian exile was a purifying force in the world-view of Israel, the reflective return to tradition was not a regressive process. As the people strove to recover a more accurate understanding of what their past had meant, they also deepened their insight into their own historical role. Nowhere is this more apparent than in the "servant" passages in the second part of the book of Isaiah.

We know nothing about the great prophet who is responsible for the middle portion (chapters 40 to 55) of the book of Isaiah, except for the fact that he shared in the Babylonian exile and, as his words indicate, that he was a voice of hope for the people. Lacking any details of his identity, even his name, biblical scholars now refer to him as "Deutero-Isaiah" (Second Isaiah).

Essentially these chapters in Isaiah, sometimes referred to as "the book of consolation," are a promise of return to Jerusalem. To that extent they foresee some resumption of the role the people had previously played. But in what are perhaps the deepest religious insights of Old Testament times the prophet probes the nature of Israel's role in history.

Israel's role is seen in the light of the prophetic role itself — not too surprising a view to come from a prophet! Israel is the servant of Yahweh, not just in the sense of cultic service, but in the function of carrying Yahweh's word to the nations. Among all the nations of the world Israel is meant to bear witness to the greatness of Yahweh's name,

to his glory and his power. Israel's own history is to manifest the mercy and fidelity of her god.

The prophets of Israel, however, had generally witnessed
to Yahweh in the midst of their own persecution and suffering. Rejected because of the word of God that they bore,
they nonetheless proclaimed that word. And because that
word was a word of power — power of life to those who
received it in openness of heart, power of death to those
who refused it in their pride and stubbornness — the prophet
was the agent of Yahweh's influence over history. So, too,
says Deutero-Isaiah, is the role of Israel: The people are
to bear Yahweh's word in the world, despite rejection and
suffering. Their suffering will bear witness to Yahweh. Even
more enigmatically, their suffering will be a source of redemption for all mankind.

Here we find an insight into the dynamics of human
history that can make sense only through religious faith.
Suffering, rejection, and failure will contribute in unique
fashion to the advance of man if these experiences are lived
in witness to God. Out of the experience of death there will
somehow emerge a growth in life. Already in the pages of
Deutero-Isaiah we find the paradoxical mystery of death
and new life, the same mystery we find in the death and
resurrection of Jesus of Nazareth. One may reject this insight
as a principle for interpreting human history, but one cannot
deny its uniqueness. Nor can one deny that even for Deutero-
Isaiah this view could have absolutely no foundation apart
from Israel's faith in the fidelity and transcendent power of
its god, Yahweh.

Apart from his teaching on the role of suffering, Deutero-
Isaiah marks an advance in Israel's understanding of the
process by which time is to be sacralized. Yahweh himself is
still seen to be the principal source of this sacralization, by
the fact of his guiding presence in Israel's life. Yet, in the
view of Deutero-Isaiah, there is a special role that the people
of Israel themselves play in making human history a sacred

reality. If Israel bears the word of Yahweh in its faith and traditions, it is not solely for Israel's sake; Israel is to make that word present to the consciousness of other nations, so that their experience also may be transformed. Israel should be a prophetic people, testifying before all peoples to the fact that Yahweh is the Lord of history.

No matter how profoundly one reflects on the meaning of history, it is something that must not only be thought about but lived. So, when the opportunity to return to Jerusalem and to rebuild it came, with the decree of Cyrus in 538 (which directed the restoration of Jerusalem), Deutero-Isaiah urged the deportees to return. Drawing from the ancient traditions of Israel's liberation from Egypt, the prophet describes the return from Babylonian exile as a new exodus, even more glorious than the first exodus, for now Yahweh himself will lead back his people to the promised land. The new era that the returning exiles face, the period of reconstruction and of the establishment of Judaism, is related in its origins to the traditions of Israel.

Actually, the facts connected with the reconstruction of Jerusalem and its Temple are hard to ascertain, and therefore it is perilous to pass any judgment on the faith-attitudes of the Jews during those unsettled centuries. Certainly there was some retention of the messianic expectancies, as the book of Zechariah testifies, but in the absence of any kings on the throne of David it is hard to say what those messianic passages meant to the people of those days. The fundamental traditions of Israel were certainly cherished and passed on from one generation to another in Temple and synagogue, where reading from "the law and the prophets" became a regular practice. But somehow (and probably falsely) one gets the impression that the pace of Israel's intrinsic development slowed down during the post-exilic period. Prophetism disappeared from the life of the people. Instead there grew up the scribal movement, essentially devoted to commenting on sacred texts already in existence rather than to communicating a new and fresh word of God to men.

Priesthood, of course, flourished with the rebuilding of the Temple, and the high priesthood even took over some of the aura and the trappings of the absent kingship. But both the liturgy and the life of those centuries seem strangely insular. Jerusalem seems almost to be dwelling in its own little world, out of touch with the history that was developing around it. Tradition was almost more of a process of clinging to the past glories of Israel (which, of course, looked much more glorious from a distance!), than of recalling the past in order to challenge the present. This was not totally the case, of course, because the celebration of the great feasts, such as Passover, always gave each new generation the opportunity to enter into and identify with the experience of their faith-ancestors.

The Apocalyptic Perspective

Something did change, though, in the attitude of the Jews towards history, and one can see this change reflected in the current of thought referred to as "apocalypse." The apocalyptic movement in Jewish literature, as in other ancient literatures, was characterized by certain stylistic features such as the "revelation" of certain hidden truths, usually detailed predictions "ex eventu"; a highly involved use of allegorical imagery; fascination with numbers. More important for the present discussion is the attitude toward time and history that marks apocalyptic thought. Fundamentally, the present context of history is repudiated, is judged incapable of evolving into fulfillment, and "salvation" is reserved for some extra-temporal situation that will follow the utter destruction of the present world.

It is interesting to note that apocalyptic writing is scarcely represented in the canon of Old Testament scriptures. There are traces of apocalyptic style in Ezekiel. The book of Daniel comes closest to being a book of apocalypse, but even it is not in its mentality a thoroughgoing example of apocalypse.

However, the apocalyptic cast of mind was prevalent during those centuries immediately before the Christian era. Pessimistic with regard to human history, it looked for man's hope only in "the beyond." Perhaps in Israel's case this attitude was fortified by the continued disappointments experienced by her people.

For many decades after their resettlement of Jerusalem, life was peaceful for the returned exiles. Though they enjoyed neither power nor great affluence, they were relatively autonomous in the regulation of their own life. Persian rule was not overly oppressive as far as we can ascertain. The division of Alexander's empire after his death in 323 left the Jews temporarily under the control of the Ptolemies, who did not noticeably interfere with their life.

Things changed when the Seleucid kings wrested Palestine from the Ptolemies toward the end of the third century. The process of Hellenization, that had already been deeply though gently felt during the previous hundred years, was now greatly accelerated by the Seleucid rulers, who were fanatically intent on "enriching" their subject peoples with Greek culture. Under Antiochus Epiphanes IV, who came to power in 175 B.C., matters came to a head. Not only was political and military domination the order of the day, but the cult of Greek religion was imposed upon the reluctant Jews. Once more the very existence of the chosen people was threatened.

Confronted with this danger to their faith and their life, the Jews revolted and, under the leadership of the Macabees, managed to throw off the Seleucid yoke. For a time they enjoyed relative freedom and self-rule, but when the armies of Pompey marched through the Near East in 66 B.C. the Jews once more come under foreign domination, this time by the Romans.

It is not surprising that the chosen people should have

grown somewhat disillusioned with the processes of history, and that in their disillusionment they should have felt an affinity for the apocalyptic thought that was so widespread in the Mediterranean world at that time. Perhaps the promises made by Yahweh — for even their understanding of apocalypse is transformed by the traditional faith in Yahweh — cannot be fulfilled in this world of time and space, and can find realization only in some heavenly "kingdom of the saints." This would seem to be the burden of the book of Daniel, which is so obviously influenced by the events of the Maccabean period.

To the extent, however, that later Jewish thought adopted this apocalyptic perspective it was abandoning the classic eschatology of the great prophets of Israel. Jewish apocalypse remains basically optimistic regarding the fidelity of Yahweh: Yahweh is the holy one of Israel who will not abandon his people; he has proved himself not only faithful but also merciful; in a final "day of the Lord" Israel will be led in triumph to a heavenly kingdom. But the apocalyptic writings are less optimistic about human history as it unfolds on this earth. Their hopes for Israel's future lie precisely in the expectation of a *heavenly* kingdom. Salvation, then, will ultimately be found beyond time and space. And this present world? Having served as the place where Israel could work out her long exile from paradise and by fidelity to Yahweh's law gain access to the heavenly kingdom, this world will disappear in flaming destruction.

Such, obviously, was not the perspective of Israel's great prophets nor, for that matter, was it the perspective of the other major streams of Old Testament tradition. Israel's prophets were certainly not naive about human life or about man's inadequacy in living that life as he should. No voice in human history has spoken out more sharply to indict man's sinfulness than did the voice of the Old Testament prophet. Still, to the very end, Israel's prophetic movement remains fundamentally hopeful about human history. History will require salvation — even the chosen people had proved their need of help — but Yahweh is a saving god.

More than any other group in Israel, the prophets saw the intrinsic law of justice that demanded the punishment of their people's infidelity. They speak of even the land sharing in the downfall and chastisement of the people. The land (and Jerusalem especially) will also share in the blessing of restoration. Some of the prophets use paradise imagery in speaking about this future day of restoration, and they apply this imagery to the land of Israel itself — it will be made by Yahweh into a "paradise regained." And for the two great prophets of exile, Ezekiel and Deutero-Isaiah, the center of this regained paradise will be Jerusalem.

None of Israel's prophets thought that the "day of the Lord" had arrived. When it did come, some time in the future, it would be a "new thing" but it would also stand in continuity with the history in which Israel was already involved; it would be the final outcome of the saving process that Yahweh was already directing through Israel's historical evolution. For that very reason, reflection upon the traditions that recalled Yahweh's great deeds of the past was a means of discerning, even though faintly, the pattern of the future.

This is exactly what the prophetic "theology of history" does: The prophet stands before Israel, challenging his contemporaries to conversion, i.e. to a radical decision about the present, a decision to ally with Yahweh in facing the demands of the present moment. As guidelines for this conversion the prophets propose the traditions of the past and the hope for a "day of the Lord." Understanding of Yahweh's present action, and correlatively of the action demanded of Israel, is polarized by recollection of Yahweh's previous saving acts and by expectation of his future achievement of salvation.

The prophetic word, which the prophets claim to be "the word of the Lord," is always a call to something *new*. It cannot be otherwise. Not only is each generation faced with new circumstances that demand decisions, but thoroughgoing acceptance of Yahweh would be something new, something Israel had never really experienced. On the other hand the prophetic word is radically *traditional*. The prophet's aim was to recall a forgetful people to the god who had proved his loving care for them by the great things he had already done on their behalf. Israel's prophets had a deep involvement in the problems of their day, even though some of them (Jeremiah, for example) longed to avoid that involvement. They also had a deep sense of history. Because they did, our own sense of history is, or at least can be, greatly enriched.

There is much we can learn by studying the world-view of Israel's prophets. If nothing else, we can learn to avoid a facile designation of present-day thinkers as either "traditional" or "progressive." The prophets of Old Testament times were the most progressive thinkers of their own day, so much so that they aroused bitter opposition among those who wished to cling to the status quo. Yet, as we have pointed out, they were the most keenly aware of the traditions that were meant to be normative of Israel's faith and decisions.

Actually, a believing Christian today can go far beyond the vision of the Old Testament prophets. The traditions of the past on which he can ground his appraisal of the present include not only the "great deeds of Yahweh" in Old Testament times but also the life, death, and resurrection of Jesus of Nazareth who is the Christ. The day of the Lord to which he looks forward as the goal of his present-day decisions is not the hazily foreseen future that Israel's prophets anticipated; it is a sharing in the risen existence of Christ himself.

For the moment we can postpone an examination of Christian eschatology, but the very mention of it draws attention to a fundamental and unavoidable inadequacy of Old Testament reflection on the meaning of human history. One of the most critical gaps in Israel's vision of life was the lack of any satisfactory understanding of the afterlife. Israel shared with most ancient cultures a relatively unformulated conviction that men somehow continue in existence after death. In the earlier centuries of Israelitic thought, it was assumed that a person after his death went down to Sheol, the underworld. This was not a happy fate. Sheol seems to have been envisaged as a place of dreary darkness and unhappiness; the greatest blessing Yahweh could give was to preserve a person from Sheol as long as possible.

Towards the very end of Old Testament times one finds a more optimistic note, though still no great clarification. Late wisdom literature alludes to the fact that "the souls of the just are with God," which is certainly much better than being in Sheol, but there is still no real insight as to what awaited man beyond death. Earlier wisdom writing, like prophetic thought before it, had lacked even this vague expectation of "life with God" and as a result, had wrestled vainly with the problem of evil and cosmic justice.

Old Testament thought, then, and specifically prophetic thought, was polarized by a future "day of the Lord" that would see the fulfillment of Yahweh's covenant promises. But the only way in which the prophets could "foresee" this future day of salvation was by projecting into the future the essential lines of development they had discovered by reflecting on Israel's past. There was another and very important element that entered into the prophet's hope for the future: his own unique religious experience of Yahweh. This too was translated by the traditions of Israel, for the Yahweh who came in immediacy to the prophets of Israel was the same Yahweh who "led our fathers out of Egypt."

Israel, obviously, did not have a very clear idea of the future of man, or the "day of the Lord" when salvation would be accomplished. But that such salvation would eventually come, remained a firm conviction of Israel's faith. After all, Yahweh had acted and still continued to act in her life, and he did not act in vain or in deceit. He was a god who was both all-powerful and faithful.

The Scribes

More and more in the later centuries of the Old Testament period, hope for salvation centered on the law. It was in the law that Yahweh was directing his people towards salvation; it was in the law that the wisdom which belonged only to Yahweh was embodied and made present to men. One might almost say that the law began to function as the fulfillment of the messianic expectancies: it was looked upon as the force in Israelitic society that would bring about peace and justice; it was the mediator by means of which Yahweh himself ruled his people and watched over them.

Israel's chief task lay in the observance of the law. To help bring that about, there grew up in post-exilic Judaism a group of legal experts, the scribes, whose function was to interpret for the people the precise dictates of the law.

It is instructive to compare the activity of these scribes with that of the charismatic prophets, for the comparison tells us much about the nature of religious faith and practice. Both scribe and prophet are teachers of the people. Both have for their object the kind of practical understanding that will lead to conversion and salvation; both are trying to interpret "the will of God." For both prophet and scribe the traditions of Israel are sacred and a norm for any decision that the present demands.

To make a somewhat over-simplified judgment, however, the prophet looks more to *events* whereas the scribe looks more to a *book*. Faced with critical times that require a basic response to Yahweh in faith, the prophet recalls to the people the great things that their god has done for them. He recalls the covenant promises this god has made and his fidelity to his promises. And he urges the people, in particular the leadership of Israel, to choose a course of action based upon dependence on this god. The prophets are aware of Israel's law and they urge the people to observe it. But they are wary of the superficial externalism that would be content with nothing more than the legal fulfilment of the law, that would be content with "not breaking the law."

One must be careful not to level an unqualified charge of "legalism" against the scribal movement, for the scribes were certainly aware of the fact that Yahweh demanded more than purely extrinsic observance of the law. When a group of men are professional students and interpreters of a formulated law, however, the danger of legalism is real. Once something is written, it can become fixed and static, and this is much truer of precise legal language than it is of poetry.

There seems to be a fair amount of historical evidence that the scribes of Judaism did not thoroughly avoid this danger; that, for some at least, observance of the law almost became an end in itself. For them the law tended to become the key to Jewish (and indirectly to human) history. To the extent that the Jews observed the law, history would move towards its fulfillment. It was in the law that Yahweh made himself present to his people; it was in the law that he communicated to them his own wisdom. The giving of this law was *the* great deed that Yahweh had worked for the salvation of his chosen people.

Important as it became in Jewish faith and life, the law never replaced Yahweh. The religion of Israel, with all its ups and downs, was definitely Yahwistic and, as such, unique among the religions of ancient man. The experience of faith and of human life was different for the Israelites because space and time were dominated for them by the powerful yet merciful presence of their god. Whether one accepts the faith of Israel and says that God did transform the experienced history of this people, or whether one rejects that faith and studies Israel simply as another historical phenomenon, the ascertainable historical fact is that their faith and religious insights did make their history different from that of other peoples.

For Christians, the Israelitic faith-experience of living in sacralized space and time is critically important, because it prepares for Jesus of Nazareth and therefore for Christianity.

In Christian faith, it is the death and resurrection of Jesus that gives to the cosmos and to history a radically new principle of sacralization. In his death and resurrection Jesus becomes Lord of history and master of the created universe. But he who did so, brought into the transforming experience of death and resurrection his own Jewish faith and traditions. In him the religious experience of the chosen people grows into the experience of Easter. There is a profound link between the religious faith and traditions of Israel and those of Christians. To understand that link, one must answer the basic question posed to Christians (and by them to others): Who is Jesus of Nazareth?

CHAPTER FOUR

The Gospel of Life

IT WOULD BE difficult to find a passage in English literature that is more widely remembered and quoted than the famous soliloquoy, "To be or not to be," from Shakespeare's *Hamlet*. Probably the reason for the widespread appeal of this passage is that the poet, with his gift for capturing what is universal in human experience, has expressed mankind's most basic quest: the search for meaningful existence, the search for real life.

Men have searched for many things: for wealth, comfort, power, fame, for that elusive reality called "happiness." But basic to all these is the search for the key to continuing life, since all these other goals have meaning only if one *is*. Not that sheer continuation in existence is sufficient; men wish to *live* in the full sense of that term.

History indicates that men have always puzzled over the "afterlife." And the views that individual men or cultures have taken regarding a future life cover a wide spectrum. Many have looked forward to it with a vague trepidation, fearing the unknown; others have imagined it as a situation of final retribution, of reward for the good and punishment for the wicked; some have denied the very possibility of such a future life; while still others have been openly agnostic, seeing no evidence for or against another life. One thing seems clear: Men have never been able to free themselves from questions about immortality, nor have they been able to stop searching for some way of overcoming the enigma of human death.

Our modern world is no exception. Despite the many differences that distinguish man today from his predecessors on earth, the basic human desires and searches seem, in the last analysis, to remain very much the same. Even though the forms devised to preserve and improve human existence differ drastically from what they were even fifty years ago — to say nothing of fifty thousand years ago — the drive to find, preserve, and develop life is still at the root of most human activity.

Ancient literature such as the Babylonian story of Gilgamesh, or the Egyptian burial texts, testifies to the fact that men were constantly searching for immortality. It is no less the case today. Modern man is spending his time, his energy, and his genius on the means of discovering the secret of life. Ancient man, of course, tried to find this secret through mythology and magic; we moderns carry on our research in more sophisticated fashion through the "myth" and "magic" of science and medicine. But fundamentally, are we not still eagerly searching, hopefully seeking, the secret that will unlock the doors of death and give man the unending life he desires?

In one respect, however, the quest for life in the contemporary world is different from what it was in some more primitive periods of history. Man today realizes that only when he lives in freedom is his existence really human. Obviously, this is not an entirely new concept. For many centuries there has been a slow advance in man's emphasis on freedom, an advance accelerated in the last two centuries by the series of revolutions that began with the American Revolution of 1776. Now we are witnessing a worldwide explosion of consciousness that freedom is indispensable to genuine human life. Our world is being rocked by this explosion. Peoples long accustomed to living in subjection, to accepting their enslavement with relative submission, are no longer content with this dehumanizing situation. The quest for freedom is dominating human life from one end of the world to the other, and it is touching every aspect of life: political, economic, social, familial, religious.

How realistic, though, are these expectations of freedom? How can we achieve genuine freedom for all men? Recent experience seems to say that the very forces or movements that promise liberation bring with them their own form of enslavement. No factor of modern life has done more to free men than the advance of technology; yet it has also brought with it the threat of a computerized, mathematically programmed, dehumanized future. Our exciting advances in communications can and should be a major influence in freeing men, but the monopolistic control of these media can mean a frightening destruction of freedom through world-wide brainwashing. Genuine political self-determination becomes more difficult as governmental processes increase in complexity. We have seen Marxist revolutions destroy the oppressive structures of serfdom, only to result in their own forms of despotism.

Strangely, despite the unprecedented potential for advance that we possess today, our world is gripped by a crisis of hope. We see this reflected in much of the literature, the art, and the theater of the times. Even the revolutionary movements of the day are often motivated more by desperation than by optimistic expectancy. The question, then, is a real one: Is it possible for men to attain true human life, life that is free and meaningful, life that will continue into unending fulfillment after death?

The Key to Life and Freedom

To this question Christianity replies with a clear "yes." If Christianity has any meaning for human life, it is precisely in providing this unique and all-important answer. This claim to possess an ultimate answer to freedom and life can, certainly, sound arrogant and naive. And if the claim cannot be justified, Christians deserve to be condemned for deceiving their fellowmen with vain and frustrating hopes. But if the claim is true, if the Christian community does possess the key to unending personal freedom and life, there is the definite possibility that the positive promise of our present world-situation can be realized and the dangers averted. Put simply, the Gospel of Jesus Christ may be critically relevant today.

This much is undeniable: From its origins Christianity has been a straightforward confrontation of the questions of freedom and immortality. The very existence of Christianity is rooted in the unique experience of a small group of people, an experience in which they suddenly and unexpectedly discovered the key to life and freedom. This was the Easter experience of Jesus' immediate disciples.

This discovery necessarily took place in the context of faith. Only those who believed in Christ experienced him in his risen situation, and the exact nature of that experience is most difficult to ascertain. In our own day, those who would subscribe to the reality of that original Christian experience must themselves admit that the answer to life provided by the resurrection of Jesus is one that can be grasped only in faith and realized only in hope. It is impossible, outside the context of faith, to give any "proof" (or for that matter, any disproof) for the resurrection of Jesus. All one can do by careful historical study is to examine the faith of the earliest followers of Jesus, the impact of that faith on the origins of Christianity, and the historical development of the community of faith (the Church) which has retained and refined that faith through the past two millenia.

Granted that such careful study of the historical phenomenon of the Christian community may be unsatisfactory, in that it leaves the factual question about the resurrection of Jesus unanswered, it still is study of great value. At the very least it will give the believer an educated understanding of what it is he is believing; and it will give the unbeliever an educated understanding of what he is rejecting.

In beginning this study it seems important to stress the fact that Christianity did begin with an *experience,* with an *event.* To this extent it stands in continuity with Israel's historical orientation towards faith and religion. Israel had come into being through the experienced events of exodus, covenant, and conquest of the land (the word "event" in this context refers not just to the external happening — entering the land of Canaan by crossing the Jordan — but to that event as experienced by a group of people. Such, also, was the origin of Christianity, though in its case the historical circumstances of the experience can be more definitely located.

The original Christian community in Jerusalem did not begin as an organized body of people brought together by clear objectives, establishing itself in a structured way of life in order to attain those objectives. What seems to have happened is this. A group of men and women who had come to know Jesus of Nazareth and who had increasingly believed that he was to be the Messiah of Israel, had had their hopes and dreams utterly shattered by the official Jewish repudiation of Jesus and by his death at the hands of the Roman executioners. Then came the totally unexpected, the undreamed-of reversal: this Jesus now revealed himself to them, not as dead, but as alive; not so much "come back to life" as passed into a new way of existing that was human but radically transformed; not just the Messiah of Israel, but the human translation of the lordship of God himself. This risen Jesus was now both Messiah and Lord.

It was this experience that bound them together, no longer in fear and defensiveness (as they had been driven together by the trial and death of their leader), but as people who had shared something absolutely shattering and unprecedented. Literally, there was no one else to whom they could turn to share what had now become the deepest level of their understanding of life. Because they believed that the risen Christ continued to be with them, and his presence dominated their consciousness, they felt a most intimate bond with one another.

Some of the earliest recollections of Christianity's beginnings are reflected in the first few chapters of the Acts of the Apostles. Here we are told how, without much planning or organization, the early Christians began to gather together to share their lives and their earthly goods, to be formed by the teaching of the apostles, and — most importantly — to share with one another the commemoration of Christ's death and resurrection through the eucharistic breaking of bread (Acts 2:42).

It would be a mistake, grounded in a superficial reading of the New Testament literature, to think that the early Christians were bound together in community simply by something that *had* happened. Unquestionably the experiences of Holy Week were basic and set the pattern, but they flowed into the continuing experience of the early Christians, their continuing experience of the risen Christ and of his Spirit. For them this was the experience of a new life, a new life into which they had already entered because of their relationship with the risen Lord, a new life that they were meant to foster and develop, a new life that would flow unbroken beyond death. Already they possessed the beginning of "eternal life," because the risen Christ remained present to them and shared with them what he already was.

As far as we can gather, the early Christians almost immediately began to spread the "good news" of Jesus' resurrection. Logically, they began with their fellow-Jews in Jerusalem, bringing them the message that this Jesus whom they had experienced as a man in their midst — and whom their leaders had put to death — had through his death and resurrection opened up the secret of human life. Because this Jesus was now alive and sharing in the power of his Father who had raised him up from death, mankind was no longer ultimately subject to the powers of death and chaos and sin. Because he has thus redeemed mankind, Jesus should be recognized as both Messiah and Lord (Acts 3:11-26).

Spreading out from Jerusalem, the early Christians went to Damascus and Antioch, to Joppa and Caeserea, and then quickly to most of the important cities of the Mediterranean world. Everywhere, as their traditions recall, they preached the good news of the Lord Jesus — the startling message of his resurrection — and with it the promise of a share in this new life for all who would accept the Gospel in faith.

In those early decades their acceptance, either in the Jewish communities of the Roman world or in non-Jewish circles, was not very broad. And the message they preached — the death and resurrection of Jesus — proved an unacceptable enigma to most of their hearers (Acts 17:22-33). As Paul himself wrote to the Christian community at Corinth, the Gospel of Jesus' resurrection was a stumbling-block to the Jews and foolishness to the Gentiles (1 Cor. 1:22-25). Yet slowly the numbers of believers began to grow, and within little more than two centuries Christianity had become a major social force in the Roman Empire.

As the early Christians preached the good news of Christ's resurrection, they inevitably reflected more deeply on the meaning of this event. Even more so, as they explained to new converts the fuller implications of this new faith and life they had embraced, these early Christian communities were forced to clarify and develop their own understanding of Jesus. Who was he? What had he done? What was he still doing? The *kerygma,* the basic proclamation of the good news that Jesus had risen from death and was therefore to be recognized as Messiah and Lord, was thus complemented by the *catechesis.* We can obtain a good idea of what this catechesis was, since it formed the early Christian traditions out of which the New Testament literature developed.

The New Testament bcoks, particularly the four Gospels, indicate that the faith and theological reflection of the early Christian communities centered on Jesus himself. Jesus was the one who had overcome the age-old riddle of death; and he had done so as a man, by the simple yet stupendous action of passing through death into new human life. Moreover he had overcome death (and with it all evil), not by some kind of magic or physical might, but by that which is proper to a man as a person: by his love and free decision (Phil. 2:5-11).

The early Christians did not develop any technical explanation of the manner in which Jesus' human psychological activity was causative of salvation, but they were clear and explicit about the fact that Jesus overcame evil and saved men by his obedience. Precisely because he freely accepted the dictates of his historical role — that of a servant Messiah — Jesus becomes the Lord of salvation in his resurrection. Because he resisted the temptation to avoid being a suffering Messiah, because he gave himself in love to men even unto death, he is revealed in his resurrection as the Lord of life. Thus the gift to mankind of unending life is rooted in Jesus' use of his freedom.

In many ways the early Christian faith in the resurrection of Jesus is a radical break with the past. For Christians the event of Easter began a new era in human existence; it was the beginning of a new creation, it inaugurated a new mankind (Eph. 2:14-18). What happened in the death and resurrection of Jesus was not simply the fuller development of what had gone before, not even in the history of Israel. The event of Jesus — his human life, death, and resurrection — introduced into the consciousness of the early Christians a principle of radical discontinuity. It challenged every understanding they had had of man, of the world, and of God. The more they reflected on the event, the greater the challenge became.

Continuity with Israel

Despite this basic discontinuity between Judaism and the new reality that began with Jesus, the first Christians saw that there was also an important link between what we today call the Old and New Testaments. Coming out of a profoundly Jewish background (the earliest Christian communities were predominantly Jewish) the first Christians logically viewed the mystery revealed in Jesus' resurrection as the fulfillment of all that Yahweh had done for his people in the preceding centuries. The resurrection was the great decisive act of Yahweh in liberating his people.

Throughout the Old Testament period, the action of God had been seen as one of liberating the people from evil, which was appropriately symbolized by death. The great exemplary experiences of exodus and exile made it absolutely clear that God did not wish his own people to die historically, but to rise up again to new and fuller life. This seems clearly to be the meaning of the famous vision of Ezekiel in which he saw the valley strewn with the dry bones, a symbol of defeated and exiled Israel; and then saw the bones come together, take on sinew and skin, and stand once more as a mighty army, the symbol of Israel revivified by the word and the spirit of Yahweh (Ezek. 37).

As Israel's faith developed there was the increasing insight of her people that the god they worshipped was a god of life. One of the most prominent appellations of God in the Old Testament is "living god." This means not only that he himself is alive, in contrast to the dead pagan idols of wood and stone, but that he is the unlimited source of life and power (Is. 40:12-23). As such, he is the hope of Israel.

God's promise of life, which Israel's traditions recall as a constant and repeated promise, was understood primarily in terms of Israel's historical continuation in existence. There was also increasing insight into the fact that God did not simply want his people to avoid extinction; he wanted them to grow qualitatively, becoming ever more conscious of him and his love, deepening their fidelity and dedication, living in greater peace and justice.

Even when the people were chastised for their infidelity, apparently carried off to slavery and death, God did not abandon his own. Through the great prophets there comes the promise of a "day of the Lord" that will be a day of restoration; Israel will rise again to new life and freedom. To the Jews of Jesus' day, looking back on the traditions of their history, this promise of restoration to life had been verified in the Jewish return from Babylon and the consequent rebuilding of Jerusalem and its Temple. When they gathered in the Temple to celebrate the great festival of Tabernacles, which commemorated both the exodus and the return from exile, they sang in reference to that restoration: "This is the day that the Lord has made. . . . "

To the early Christians, the divine liberation that found expression in these Old Testament events comes to fulfillment in the Father's act of raising Jesus from death to new life. Easter is truly and fully "the day that the Lord has made" (Ps. 118).

Much of Israel's hope for restoration was tied to the promise Yahweh had made to David. David himself was God's "anointed" (Messiah), and later generations in the kingdom of Judah kept hoping that the successors of David would also prove to be "Yahweh's anointed." With very few exceptions, however, they were a bitter disappointment. As a result, the expectation of a true Messiah was projected further into the future, and the figure of this coming Messiah was increasingly idealized.

Along with "messianism" in the strict sense, that is the expectation of a kingly figure, a dynastic descendant of David, who would save and reestablish Israel, the later centuries of Old Testament times developed an extended "messianism." There was widespread hope that God would one day raise up a great prophet to lead the people. In some circles (as we know from the writings of the Qumran community) there was the expectation of a priestly personage who would effect the salvation of the people. By the time of Jesus, there had grown up a rather complex and diversified expectation of a Messiah, of one "who was to come" as the agent of God's saving action.

For the early Christians, Jesus, as fully realized in his death and resurrection, was seen to be the realization of Israel's messianic hopes. True, he fulfilled these hopes in a manner quite different from that anticipated, for "his kingdom is not of this world." Nevertheless, he is the great prophet who brings the prophetic vocation to its highest expression; he is the scion of David who comes to establish a new order of justice and peace; he is a new Moses who proclaims a new law and effects a new covenant.

Jesus' resurrection is the final and greatest sign of God's fidelity, the unmistakable "word" that God would never forget his promises, even in face of Israel's repeated sinfulness. From the time of the ancient patriarchs onward, Yahweh had promised life to his people. Now, with the resurrection of Jesus, new and everlasting life had broken into human history. Now the promise of life is seen as absolutely irrevocable, for the risen Jesus is that life, and a share in it is open to any man who will receive the reality of the risen Christ in faith (Jn. 6:29).

Old Testament revelation had always been a message of God's freeing action, a freeing from the forces of chaos and evil that would destroy life. In the Gospel, that is in the proclamation of Christ's resurrection, the early Christians announced the full dimension of that message. The sacred traditions of Israel are caught up into the traditions of Christianity.

Formation of the Tradition

It is most instructive for anyone who studies the history of religion, and especially so for a believing Christian, to examine the manner in which Christian tradition came into being. Although, it is impossible to discover the exact details of this process — and contemporary scholars are divided in their attempts to reconstruct those details — there is a great deal that can be said with reasonable certainty, based on a study of the New Testament texts.

Though in its finished literary form the book of the Acts of the Apostles is not the earliest book of the New Testament, it does seem to draw from some of the earliest recollections of the infant Christian community. And in the early chapters of Acts the sermons preached by Peter and Stephen and Paul are particularly interesting. Obviously, we do not have an exact record of the talks given by these men, but these passages do seem to provide a clear reflection of the earliest form of the kerygma, the announcing of the good news of resurrection to those who had not yet accepted Christ in faith.

In such texts we are apparently at the very heart of the tradition as it started to develop. Their message is brief, simple, clear, and absolutely startling: Jesus of Nazareth, a man who had lived and taught and worked in the midst of those being addressed, and who had been rejected and put to death in Jerusalem, has risen from the dead. In his resurrection he is shown to be the awaited one of Israel, the Messiah, and the very Lord of creation and history. In its earliest stages this kerygmatic preaching did not enter into any lengthy clarification of what it meant to say that Jesus was Messiah and Lord. More important than any theological explanation was the fact that this was true — and it was the function of the Apostles to witness to this event. After all, they had experienced the presence of the risen Christ in those days immediately following his death; they had shared in some way in his own experience of risen life; and to this resurrection experience they bore testimony for any who would hear their Gospel.

Distinctively different as was the immediate Easter experience of Jesus' close disciples, this sensible manifestation (whatever it was) was not the only experience of Christ's presence that the early Christians had. They seemed to have been aware of a continuing presence of the risen Christ in their midst, a presence that was connected to the Christian assembly itself — "where two or three are gathered together in my name, I am there in their midst." And this presence of the risen Lord was specially felt when they gathered for the eucharistic "breaking of the bread."

As men and women responded to the kerygma, were converted to the risen Christ, and initiated into the Christian community through the ritual of baptism, the need for further instruction arose. These new Christians, unlike Jesus' own disciples, had not historically experienced Jesus or the events of Holy Week, and so the implications of Christ's death and resurrection had to be spelled out in greater detail. Thus a regular process of catechesis, essentially an explanation of Christ's death and resurrection, began to develop.

Undoubtedly, this catechesis took various forms and occurred in many different situations. However, there is evidence that a privileged context for this early Christian instruction was the eucharistic meal of the communities. How frequently this occurred we do not know, but apparently with some regularity they gathered together — perhaps in the early evening — to celebrate a meal together. This would begin with the eucharistic breaking of bread and conclude with eucharistic sharing of the wine. In between, there would have been a sharing of their recollections about Jesus of Nazareth, a sharing of their insights into his words and deeds. Such community meals, framed by what we would call the "consecration" of the bread and wine and "reception of communion," would have been a natural occasion for instructing the faith of the newly converted. It would also have been the natural occasion for Jesus' own disciples to recall lovingly the experience they had had of their Master.

Just as in early Old Testament days the cultic celebrations at Israel's various shrines provided an important context in which the traditions were preserved and developed and the Old Testament scriptures began to come into existence, so in the early decades of Christianity the celebration of the Eucharist was a foremost occasion for the Apostles to share with their fellow Christians their faith in and experience of the death and resurrection of Jesus. Out of this apostolic catechesis there gradually developed the body of literature we call "the New Testament."

For several decades before the text of the New Testament was crystallized into the form we know, the process of tradition was carried on in this more flexible form. Most likely, there were very early written collections which eventually were incorporated into books like the four Gospels, but these were always accompanied by the oral teaching. Moreover, it would be a mistake to think that the process of oral tradition came to a halt when the New Testament literature was finally produced and accepted as official. Indispensable as is the book of New Testament scripture, the Christian celebration of the Eucharist has remained throughout the life of the Church the principal instrument of tradition.

The Experience of New Life

It would take a lengthy and complicated discussion to justify thoroughly that claim for the eucharistic action, but it might be good to reflect that Christianity in its origins, and therefore in its authentic transmission, was not a message but an experience, the experience of the new life into which the risen Jesus entered as "the first-born from the dead." Tradition cannot be for Christians a matter of handing on from generation to generation an understanding of what Jesus did; it must be an action of communicating to each new group of believers the living reality of the risen Christ himself — which is what Christians believe happens in the Eucharist.

All of this presupposes a certain understanding of what resurrection is, or more precisely what the resurrection of Jesus is. One can speak of resurrection as an event or a happening, and the early Christians do just this. Yet the concrete reality of resurrection as they speak of it in faith is the risen Christ himself; he is the resurrection and the new life (Jn. 11:25). We might, then, look at the faith of the early Christian communities and ask the question: What did they think the reality of risen life meant for Jesus himself?

One thing is clear: They were convinced that he was *alive.* For them this was not a question of his memory living on among his disciples, or of his unique influence continuing to shape their lives, or of his teaching being retained as a living inspiration for all future generations. *He* was himself alive. He had truly died on Calvary, but now he was no longer dead.

Moreover, though they believed that the risen Christ lived with a new life, never before experienced by man, this was definitely *human* life. In their theological reflection they would go on to probe the divine dimension of Christ, but this did not diminish their realization that he was truly man, even in his glorified life. Actually, his passage into resurrection achieved the fullness of his manhood, which was his human destiny. And his new human existence was a fully embodied one. Though, obviously, Christ's bodily existence was drastically changed, there is no indication that the early Christians thought of the risen Jesus as a disembodied spirit, as an "angelized" man. Belief in the bodiliness of the risen Christ made possible for the early Christians their understanding of the Church as body and their faith in the eucharistic presence of the risen Christ.

Christ was himself a living example, in many respects the classic example, of the religious problem of continuity and discontinuity. The risen Christ, known only in faith by those who believed in him, was the same Jesus whom his disciples had known in his historical existence, the Jesus they had heard and seen and touched. He was also quite different. He had passed into glorification; he was no longer subject to death or to anything connected with death; he was no longer circumscribed by the limitations of earthly time and space. He had become trans-historical.

This is not to say that the early Christians viewed the resurrection of Christ as an act in which he *left* them. True, the events of his arrest and trial and death had been an experience of loss for his disciples, but Easter had been the experience of rediscovery, of regaining him. In his resurrection Jesus had "gone to his Father," but this understanding of the early Church does not seem to militate against her consciousness of his abiding presence with them. Unavoidably, the passage of Jesus into risen life involved an important element of removal, for his disciples could no longer experience him in the tangible fashion they had known earlier. There seems, however, to have been little, if any, of the view of later centuries that the risen Christ had "gone up to heaven." Instead, the risen Christ remains present to space and time, transforming them from within by his activity in human lives, and thus bringing to fulfillment the sacralization of man's experience.

Finally — and this is closely linked with early Christian faith in Christ's abiding presence — the risen life of Christ is looked upon as a life of increased activity; with his resurrection he enters into his full saving effectiveness. While he was on earth he had begun the work of man's redemption, but only with death and new life does he become fully Messiah and Lord. Contrary to the Old Testament Sabbath symbolism — God making his creation and then resting from his labors — the early Christian faith is reflected in the words of Jesus in the Gospel of John: "My Father is working still, and I am working" (Jn. 5:17).

Early Christianity's understanding of the resurrection of

Christ was, then, a very dynamic one. What had happened was a mystery of power and of life, a mystery that touched Christ in the first instance but that flowed out from him to transform all men. The experience that they had of this remarkable event left no doubt in the minds of Jesus' disciples that something had happened to them as well as to him. What this was, they only gradually came to appreciate.

Paul and the Christian Experience

While the faith of primitive Christianity was quite simple and concrete in its acceptance of the risen Christ, there began very early a process of theological reflection, an attempt to give clarification to the Easter event. In part this was simply the human tendency to seek understanding of one's experience; in part it was needed so that the early Christians could explain their faith to converts or to non-believers; in part it was required in order that faith could be translated into the practicalities of daily life; and in part it was demanded by the community's need to discover its own identity in distinction from Judaism.

In trying to trace these earliest theological developments of Christian faith, we are largely dependent upon the letters of Paul to some of the early Christian communities that he had founded, or to which he felt particularly attached, such as the community in Rome. Written over a period of fifteen years, from about 50 to 65 A.D., they reflect not only Paul's own understanding of Christ and early Christianity but also the faith of the early Church which he guided. As such they provide an invaluable insight into those critical years when the infant Church was struggling to identify its own reality, and to give some explanation of what had happened in the event of Jesus' death and resurrection.

Paul's thought was rich and profound, as even a cursory reading of his epistles makes clear. Even though his purpose in writing to the various Churches was to form their practical understanding of what it meant to live as Christians, the letters contain a wealth of theological reflection, reflection that draws from his intimate knowledge of the Old Testament, from his own Rabbinic training, and from his acquaintance with some of the non-Jewish thought of his day.

For this reason, one must beware of categorizing Paul's thought in simple fashion. However, it does seem valid to say that his approach to explaining Jesus was to concentrate on what Christ had accomplished in his death and resurrection. He is certainly eager to have his readers know who Christ really is, but even this objective is sought by explaining what Christ had done and still does. This action of Christ, as the Pauline letters describe it, is essentially one of *liberation:* Christ has freed man from the slavery of evil.

Paul's earliest letters, to the Thessalonian Christians, seem to reflect still the primitive Church's discovery that death had been overcome through the resurrection of Jesus. It is not surprising that this aspect of Christ's redeeming action so absorbed the consciousness of early Christians; if true, this piece of "good news" was certainly the most startling information that had come to the human race. Death symbolized the entire enigma of evil in human life and quite logically so, because it expressed the ultimate loss for a man of all that he cherished, especially the loss of life itself. Moreover, death seemed to make a mockery of human freedom. Death was inevitable and man was enslaved by this doom. Now, with the resurrection of Jesus, all of this was suddenly changed.

Apparently the first decades of Christianity were so caught up in the wonder of this liberation from death, that many thought the "end of the world" was imminent. Within their own lifetime the Parousia would occur, that is the risen Jesus would come in all his power and glory, put an end to history as men had known it, and inaugurate fully the final situation of triumph and unending life. There is some of this mentality in the letters to the Thessalonians, though it is not clear whether Paul himself shared this view.

Though the expectancy of an immediate Parousia was mistaken, it was grounded in a true insight (true, at least, to Christian faith): with the resurrection of Christ, the triumph of man over death had occurred. In a sense, Jesus himself had passed beyond the "end of the world" and so had those who were joined with him. Even though men, including those who had been joined by baptism to the power of Christ's resurrection, still had to pass through the experience of death, this experience now was radically transformed; it was no longer loss of life, but the passage into full human life.

All Paul's letters speak of this liberation from death, for this was a basic, enduring element of the Gospel, but very early he began to stress a more basic liberation: freedom from the root of evil, which is sin.

Paul's thought on this matter is realistic. Christ's death and resurrection have not removed sin from men's lives; even those who have been joined to Christ through baptism continue to sin, sometimes grievously. While he is insistent with his converts that a life of sin is incompatible with the new identity and new life they have, he is quite aware that they have a continuing need for conversion. One need only read the two letters to the Church of Corinth to discover how practical-minded Paul was in this regard.

Moreover, his letters, particularly the one to the Romans, deal with the puzzling, mysterious reality of sin. Sin for Paul takes on cosmic dimensions. True, sin exists because of the free choices of men, but it somehow reaches out beyond the sins of any individual or group of individuals. Sin has touched the history of mankind from its beginnings, from Adam onward (Rom. 5). While it has not deprived man of his fundamental power of moral choice, it does exercise a certain paralyzing and limiting force. It deceives and enslaves man: "I do not do the good I want, but the evil I do not want is what I do" (Rom. 7:19).

Painfully aware though he is of man's burden of sinfulness,

Paul is still fundamentally optimistic. The reason for his optimism is the mercy and graciousness of God who acts through the liberating power of Christ's death and resurrection. It was in his death that Jesus confronted the mystery of evil, triumphed over it by the force of his own love and freedom, and so broke definitively the power of sin (1 Cor. 15:20-28). By this action of supreme obedience and openness to God, Jesus introduced into human history that force that can offset — and more than offset — the enslaving power of sin (Rom. 5).

Christ's death and resurrection do not automatically remove sin from human lives, for sin touches the free decisions of men, and Christ's act is intended to increase rather than diminish man's freedom. But if a man will believe in Christ and in the power of his death and resurrection, if he will accept redemption from the risen Lord, then he has at his disposal the liberating force of Christ and his Spirit. No longer enslaved by sin, and by all that is caused by sin, a believer in Christ will live with the freedom that is appropriate to the sons of God, a true freedom of spirit that flows from the presence of Christ's own Spirit (Gal. 5).

Sin is the greatest barrier to human freedom, but there are many other influences that work to diminish freedom or make it impossible. One of the most important of these is ignorance, which is generally accompanied by elements of error and prejudice. Unless men know about the options that do exist for them in their life and experience, they are not really free to choose from among these options. One of the surest ways of enslaving people is to control their sources of information; conversely, one of the most effective means of freeing people is to inform and educate them.

The early Church was fully aware of the extent to which Christ had freed mankind by his teaching. An obvious indication of this awareness is the manner in which all four of the Gospel accounts emphasize the teaching activity of Jesus in his public ministry. Paul in his letters to the early communities sees this "illumining of mind" as extending beyond the earthly activity of Jesus; it is precisely in the vision of human life that comes with Christ's resurrection that the darkness of misunderstanding and error is dispelled. Time and again he gives thanks to God for the fact that his disciples have been illumined by the Gospel. Probably more than any of the other Apostles Paul felt this aspect of redemption, for he dealt largely and specially with the Gentiles, whose minds had not been shaped by the revelation of the Old Testament. God had drawn these Gentile converts from the darkness of their paganism into the "full light" of Christ's resurrection (Col. 1:9-14).

Again, fear, though it does not make one culpable, acts as an evil force to cripple and limit human freedom. If it becomes acute enough, fear can lead to completely compulsive activity, which is another way of saying that it removes the very possibility of free decision. In such instances a person is literally the slave of his fears. Even short of such obsessive cases of fear, there is a large area of our human decision-making that is limited because of our anxieties and worries about possible evil. If we could live without fear, or even if we could live with only reasonable fears, life would be a far freer and happier experience.

Hope is the antithesis of fear, because hope gives one the assurance that he will be able to surmount the evils that threaten him. In the emphasis on the hope that comes with the resurrection of Jesus we can see another element in the soteriology of the early Church: By his death and resurrection Christ frees men from the fears that would destroy their freedom of spirit. Perhaps what is most important, he has taken the sting of fear out of death itself. Since death is an archetypal symbol of fear in human psychology, the "defusing" of death as an evil liberates man's entire consciousness.

From beginning to end, the corpus of Pauline writing reflects this early Christian spirit of mature fearlessness.

Christians are to live in peace and to enjoy the consolation that God has given them in the resurrection of Christ. Life will have its burdens; there will even be suffering and persecution because of their faith in Christ, but from these afflictions they will be delivered and brought to life with Christ. The risen Jesus himself is their hope. His loving fidelity to them should give them the kind of deep assurance they need in order to face the risks of life.

> We know that in everything God works for good with those who love him, who are called according to his purpose. For those whom he foreknew he also predestined to be conformed to the image of his Son, in order that he might be the first-born among many brethren. And those whom he predestined he also called; and those whom he called he also justified; and those whom he justified he also glorified.
>
> What then shall we say to this? If God is for us, who is against us? He who did not spare his own Son but gave him up for us all, will he not also give us all things with him? Who shall bring any charge against God's elect? It is God who justifies; who is to condemn? Is it Christ Jesus, who died, yes, who was raised from the dead, who is at the right hand of God, who indeed intercedes for us? Who shall separate us from the love of Christ? Shall tribulation, or distress, or persecution, or famine, or nakedness, or peril, or sword? As it is written,
>
> "For thy sake we are being killed all the day long, we are regarded as sheep to be slaughtered."
>
> No, in all these things we are more than conquerors through him who loved us. For I am sure that neither death, nor life, nor angels, nor principalities, nor things present, nor things to come, nor powers, nor height, nor depth, nor anything else in all creation, will be able to separate us from the love of God in Christ Jesus our Lord.
>
> Rom. 8:28-39

It is hard for us to realize what this message of hope must have meant to Paul's hearers. Many of them seem to have been drawn from the lower levels of the social scale; many of them were slaves. For such there was little hope, humanly speaking, for a decent life. And to these people there came the Gospel, which told them that they possessed an inalienable human dignity, that their life could have lasting meaning even in the midst of human degradation, that they were loved by the God of life, who wished to bring them to unending life. Because it was a religion of hope, Christianity was from the beginning the source of a profound social revolution, a revolution that is still going on in our own day.

Paul's own special mission was to the Gentiles, to the communities that came into being beyond the more or less immediate influence of the Jerusalem mother-community. Even in these communities, however, the influence of Judaism was strong; probably a fairly large proportion of the Christians had been Jews of the Diaspora. Understandably, many of these Jewish Christians were hesitant about abandoning the attitudes and forms of their previous Jewish faith. Not only did they wish to cling to their Jewish practices themselves, but there seems to have been a strong movement to impose a Christianized Judaism on the Gentile converts. Paul reacts strongly against this, seeing in it an unjustified limitation on the freedom which the Gentiles have through Christ (Gal. 2:11-21).

Critical to this problem of "Judaizing" in the early Church was the question of the law. Probably part of the tendency of Jewish Christians to cling to the law can be attributed to a general human tendency; people hesitate to abandon patterns of life they have known. But the problem was much deeper, as we can see from the way Paul wrestles with it in his epistle to the Roman community. Any believing Jew looked upon the Old Testament law as a God-given reality, as an expression of the will of Yahweh himself. Upon the observance (or neglect) of the law the very future of Israel as a people depended. Now with the advent of Christianity the question arises: Does God no longer wish his law to be kept? Has the will of God changed from what it was in Old Testament times? Can men with impunity neglect, even abandon, this law?

Paul's response to these and similar questions, particularly in his letters to the Galatians and the Romans, is a striking witness to his faith in the liberation effected by Christ. While he recognizes the contribution of the Old Testament law to the advance of man's religious understandings, he recognizes also its inadequacies. It could make men aware of the sinfulness of certain actions, and this is of value, but it could not provide the power to avoid these actions. In a sense, it might be said to contribute somewhat to man's enslavement by sin, because it made sin a more formally conscious reality in human experience and therefore made men more painfully aware of the extent to which sin enchained them (Rom. 7:7-13).

Because the law, for all its value, was not sufficient, God has gone an all-important step beyond it in his providential guidance of mankind. His own Son become man is the new law. As such he functions as the replacement-by-way-of-fulfillment of the Old Testament law. In a later chapter we will have to examine in greater detail the manner in which the risen Christ is the law for Christians. But for the moment we can reflect on that which Paul stresses: This new situation is a profoundly liberating one. Because of the deep personal context for law in Christianity, there is no place for legalism or taboos or restrictive social customs. The Christian is meant to feel free to follow truth, to love with dedicated and mature concern for others, to worship the Father of the Lord Jesus in a manner that honestly expresses the Christian's awareness of his sonship.

One danger in legal formulations like the Old Testament laws is that they can easily lead to divisions among men. They obviously separate the people who have the law from other peoples — which need not necessarily be bad, if the people of the law can avoid a consequent judgment that they are therefore superior to other peoples. Actually, during the later centuries of the Old Testament period, the law was appealed to as support for exaggerated nationalism.

Even within Israel itself the law had some divisive effects. Some divisions, like that of men and women in Israel's ritual, were consecrated by the law. In other instances there was friction between the rigid observers of the letter of the law and those who interpreted the law's regulations in a somewhat more flexible way. To some extent, then, the Old Testament law did work against the establishment of community, whereas it should be the function of any law to foster community.

For Paul, the death and resurrection of Jesus destroyed this division: Christ has "broken down the wall of division" (Eph. 2:13-18). Within the Christian community there is to be no distinction between circumcized and uncircumcized; there is to be no distinction on the basis of eating legally "clean" or "unclean" foods; in the life of the community and in its community worship of the Father there is to be no distinction between Jew and Gentile, between rich and poor, between men and women. Christians cannot protect their prejudices by hiding behind the law; they must face one another in equality, and thus be free to form a genuine human community.

While Paul's verbal and written instruction was contributing to early Christianity's understanding of Christ's redemptive activity, another process was simultaneously at work, making its own important impact on the faith of the first-century Church. In each of the communities that was formed in those decades, the acceptance of the kerygma had to be followed up by further instruction about the meaning of Jesus' death and resurrection. Each community must have had some "program" of catechesis, even though very informal. Again, the development of a catechesis would have been more original and influential in some communities (such as those of Jerusalem or Antioch or Rome) and more derivative in others.

The Message of the Gospel

We can argue to the existence of such a process from the very nature of things, from the needs that must have arisen in these early Christian Churches. But we can also learn a considerable amount about this process by examining the similarities and differences in the four versions of the Gospel that are contained in the New Testament, since these four Gospels are in large part the product of this catechesis. Fundamentally, of course, there is one Gospel: the news of Jesus' death and resurrection. Each of the four Gospel accounts does the same thing: it gives an explanation of the meaning of Christian life, a life of faith in the continuing redemptive presence of Christ and of his Spirit, and it does so by going back to reflect on what it was that Jesus said and did in his public ministry.

All four Gospels depict Jesus as bringing life to men, but all four stress an aspect of this life-giving that is often overlooked by Christians today. Jesus communicates life to men, by his deeds and by his teaching, because *he has been sent by his Father* to do so. His Father has so loved men that he has sent his own Son as man, so that men can have life (Jn. 3:16). Jesus' teaching about his Father makes it clear that this Father is both the ultimate source and the ultimate fulfillment of the new life that comes to men through death and resurrection. In Jesus' ministry the Father is active, working to draw all men to himself. The Father, who had asked through the prophet Isaiah, "Is there anything I can do further for my vine [Israel]?" now answers that question in the parable of the caretakers of the vineyard: "What shall I do? I will send my beloved son" (Lk. 20:13).

Probably no passage in the New Testament literature is a richer reflection on this mystery of the Father giving life to men through Jesus than the sixth chapter of John's Gospel, the discourse on the bread of life. The chapter opens with an account of the multiplication of the loaves of bread, a brief description of Jesus' coming to his disciples in the storm on the Sea of Galilee, and the statement that the crowds who had witnessed the miracle of the loaves followed Jesus to Capharnaum. There they encounter him the next day in the synagogue and the remainder of the chapter is devoted to the discourse of Jesus on the bread of life.

There is no way of determining how much of the discourse as it appears in John's Gospel can be attributed to Jesus' own teaching on that occasion. The text as we have it, though rooted in Jesus' explanation of himself as the word of life, has clearly resulted from the reflection and refinement of the early Christian community and of the author of the Gospel. As such, it is a precious witness, not only to the teaching of Jesus in his public ministry, but to the faith of the first-century Church.

Jesus opens the discourse by chiding the people for their blindness. They had experienced on the previous day the multiplication of the bread, but they had failed to see what it signified; their understanding and desires had not gone beyond the level of ordinary food as the sustenance of physical life. But, says Jesus, what they should be seeking is the food that will give them unending life. And when they ask the logical question, "What do we have to do in order to get this unending life?" Jesus responds that they must accept him in faith. Remembering the catechetical origins of the Gospels, we can see how this text (when it actually came to be written) would be addressed to the early Christians. If they want the unending life that has come to men with the resurrection of Christ, what they must do as *the* key to life is believe in Jesus.

Still not taking account of the sign given them the previous day, the Jews in the Capharnaum synagogue ask Jesus what sign he can give as proof of his claim to be the source of life. Moses' claim was justified by the fact that he gave them extraordinary food: the manna, "bread from heaven." If Jesus is to demand faith in himself, he must give some comparable testimony to his mission.

The text of Jesus' response to this demand is very compressed: "It was not Moses who gave you the manna, but my Father . . .," and one would expect the sentence to finish with the words "who gave the manna," but it does not. Instead Jesus shifts the entire context of discussion into the present by saying, ". . . my Father gives you the true bread from heaven." He then goes on to point out explicitly that he is that true bread from heaven, the true source of life for men.

Behind this rapid transition of thought lies an understanding of the Old Testament "theology of the word" (and it might be worth noting that it is the Gospel of John that emphasizes Jesus' identity as Word of God). At the beginning of Old Testament history, Yahweh had manifested himself as the source of life for Israel by sustaining her existence with the extraordinary food, the manna, in the desert. Whatever actually did happen, the tradition of Israel stresses this gift of manna as the sign of Yahweh's care for his people. Apparently, however, some of the Israelites in the early centuries looked to Yahweh to support them in specially dangerous situations, but did not see him as the source of their ordinary daily living. This seems to have been the situation when they settled down in the land of Canaan. They planted crops like their Canaanite neighbors, and like them they turned to the Canaanite fertility gods to ensure the success of these crops. Yahweh might be the god of extraordinary food, but it was Baal who provided the daily bread.

It was at this point, as we mentioned earlier, that the prophet Elijah intervened, challenged the priests of Baal, and proved to the people that Yahweh was the one who provided both extraordinary and ordinary bread for them. As Israel's thought progressed further, especially in prophetic circles, the idea grew that life came from Yahweh in various ways, such as the rain bearing life to the earth, but most importantly through Yahweh's word. This word, coming through prophet and law and liturgy, carried life to anyone who would accept it. One could almost speak of this word as "bread from heaven."

It is in this context that Jesus says to the crowd at Capharnaum that he is the true bread come down from heaven. If anyone will accept in faith this Jesus, who is the word of life, he will live forever. Quite clearly the kind of life that the Father will give through Jesus, who is his word, is the life of resurrection, and this is the reason why the Father sends his Son into the world: so that men might have this unending life.

> Truly, truly, I say to you, he who believes has eternal life. I am the bread of life. Your fathers ate the manna in the wilderness, and they died. This is the bread which comes down from heaven, that a man may eat of it and not die. I am the living bread which came down from heaven; if any one eats of this bread, he will live for ever; and the bread which I shall give for the life of the world is my flesh.
>
> Jn. 6:47-51

The passage then goes on to connect the gift of life in Jesus with the eucharistic sharing in the body and blood of Christ, but the basic message remains the same: It is Jesus, now the risen Lord, who is the "true bread from heaven," because he is the Father's life-giving word. If one would live forever, he can do so by accepting the risen Christ in faith.

Clearly, then, the early Christians thought that they possessed the key to life. They could also claim to possess *wisdom* in a unique way, for the truly wise man was the one who had solved the riddle of life and death. The New Testament literature gives abundant evidence that they did claim to have this wisdom, which was not their human wisdom but the wisdom of Christ. In one of his earliest letters, his first to the Corinthian Christians, Paul tells them that they possess a paradoxical wisdom — the Gospel of life that comes through death — and that this wisdom will be rejected by both Jew and Greek (1 Cor. 1:22-25). Many will reject the proclamation of the death and resurrection of Jesus, because they will see such a solution to the riddle of life as pure foolishness. But, says Paul, to those who receive it, this word of the Gospel is power and wisdom and life.

In the Gospels, too, Jesus is depicted as the uniquely wise man. In a sense, he is wisdom itself. He solves the most difficult questions and riddles that the Scribes and Pharisees propose to him. He is wiser, not only than the trained wise men of his day, but wiser even than Solomon himself. At the source of this unparalleled wisdom is Jesus' unique relation to the Father: "... no one knows the Son except the Father, and no one knows the Father except the Son and anyone to whom the Son chooses to reveal him" (Mt. 11:27). Jesus, since he is the Son, is in immediate contact with and possession of the ultimate source of all life and all wisdom, the Father himself (Jn. 1:18).

Jesus' public ministry, as the Gospels describe it for us, was largely a matter of teaching, a communication to his disciples of that wisdom which he himself possessed. Essentially, this teaching consisted in telling men about his Father, the source and fulfillment of human life. However, Jesus' greatest revelation of wisdom came with his death and resurrection. Here, and here alone, the riddle of life and death found its solution.

The Problem of Evil

Ancient wisdom-reflection, in Israel as well as in other cultures, tried to grapple with the perennial problem of evil. Among many peoples it was a matter of trying to reconcile "cosmic justice" with the tragedies and injustices of human existence. In Israel, the problem was cast in terms of Yahweh's loving-kindness and fidelity on the one hand, and the obvious inequities of human life on the other hand. Christianity had no theoretical explanation that solves the problem of evil any more than the Old Testament had —

nor does either pretend to have. But the answer Christianity does propose is twofold: 1) the practical exhortation to work to get rid of evil in all its forms (error, ignorance, sickness, injustice, sin), and 2) the death and resurrection of Christ.

It is the second of these two "answers" that is particularly hard to accept as a realistic approach to the problem of evil. How the death and resurrection of Jesus can do anything to affect the complex and immense problems of poverty, oppression, exploitation, enslavement, and prejudice that we face in the world today seems vague at best. Yet it may just be that the only force which can ultimately lead to some solution for these human ills is personal concern and love great enough to face death for the sake of others. This, of course, is what Christian faith sees in Jesus' action of passing through death into new life. If all those who profess faith in Christ were to live out this same kind of loving commitment to the betterment of their fellow man, we would be a long step forward in overcoming evil.

Although the intrinsic power of Jesus' death and resurrection is believed to be the source of human liberation from evil, this power must be brought to bear on human life by Christians. Here we have the first of the Christian approaches to evil: get rid of it as far as possible. This is what the Gospel traditions of the early Church depict Jesus as doing in his public ministry. Out of his deep concern for people, especially for the under-privileged, he strove in every way possible to overcome the evils that afflicted them.

His teaching was itself part of this liberation from evil, since it functioned to remove the ignorance and superstition and prejudice of his contemporaries. And the heart of the message he taught was the liberation from sin and death that his Father wished to accomplish through him for men. His Father did not want human life weighed down by fears and worries, or restricted by narrow legalism. Men should have the simple openness and trust of little children.

But the message of God's concern to liberate mankind

from every form of evil was conveyed not just by Jesus' words but by the "wonders" that he worked. All four Gospels speak of these miracles of Jesus: curing the lepers, giving sight to the blind and hearing to the deaf, healing the crippled and disease-ridden, raising the dead to life again. These extraordinary deeds were obviously meant to provide a sign of the divine support for Jesus' message. However, this is only one aspect of their purpose; they were also meant to be a "word" that manifested the Father's intent to heal and free men. Jesus did these life-giving deeds as sent by his Father, and the message of the deeds, Jesus' "signs," is unmistakable: Jesus himself and his Father desire that men live and that they live freed from the burden of evil.

One of the most interesting features of the Gospel accounts of Jesus' miracles is the manner in which faith is linked with the healing that Jesus accomplishes. Again and again, he is described as demanding faith from people before he goes on to heal them. At one point it is even said that he was unable to work miracles in a certain region because the people did not believe. This seems to suggest that in the view of the early Christians (as we find this reflected in the Gospels) the life-giving power of Christ must be received in faith if it is to liberate and vivify. The word of God comes to make men free, and in so doing it does not work against a man's freedom. A man must freely choose to follow it, and if he makes this choice he will find himself increasingly free.

One thing became abundantly clear to the early Christians — and it is still unavoidably clear: Despite the death and resurrection of Jesus, the power of evil is still very strong in human experience. In fact, it seems in some ways that the potential of evil has never been so great as it is today. In the midst of this evidence how can Christians claim that evil has been overcome by the redemptive action of Christ?

Early Christianity's answer to this question, as we find it in the New Testament books, is one of faith and of hope. If one accepts the risen Jesus in faith, one accepts the promise of life and liberation that he is. His very reality as "the first-born from the dead" constitutes a promise by God to men far beyond that expressed in the Old Testament exodus and covenant, or in the Davidic dynasty. The Christian people live with a hope surpassing even that of Old Testament Israel. The fidelity of the God in whom they hope has been irrevocably proved in the resurrection of Jesus.

Christian Eschatology

"Promise and fulfillment" lie at the root of Old Testament eschatological thought. So, too, the thought of Christainity is radically eschatological, because it sees all history after Easter as working toward the fulfillment of the promise made in Jesus' passage into risen life. More radical still, the essential reality of Christianity is eschatological: the risen Christ who abides with his followers in the Church is already the Eschaton, but he has not fully accomplished in the lives of men the task of liberating them for full life. Working with the Church, as her head, the risen Lord is gradually drawing Christians – and through them all mankind – to the human fulfillment he himself enjoys. "I desire that they also, whom thou hast given me, may be with me where I am" (Jn. 17:24).

This means that the experience of Christian life is one of expectation and hope. Though the ultimate achievement of full life and freedom and joy is assured by the redeeming presence of the risen Christ and his Spirit, that achievement is still a goal towards which men must move. The future is uncertain in its concrete reality, but one element of that future is already known: the loving presence of the risen Lord, who is the witness to his Father's unfailing fidelity. How, exactly, the redemption of mankind will be worked out cannot be foreseen; but the Christian community believes that the power of divine love is such that that redemption will eventually be realized in fullness.

One could misunderstand this eschatological stance of Christianity and see it as either fatalism or quietism. If the triumph of the risen Christ is inevitable, one might look on human history as a predetermined course of events in which men are involved through no choices of their own — and Christian freedom would become an illusion. But Christians do not view the inevitability of Christ's triumph in this fashion. They trust, rather, that love, which has already in the death and resurrection of Jesus proved stronger than death and sin, will gradually overcome evil. Not just any love, of course, but the love of God that finds unlimited expression in his holy Spirit.

It is just as faulty to interpret Christian eschatology as quietistic, as if there was nothing for Christians to do in order to move history towards its destiny. True, there has been at times a trend by Christians to hold themselves aloof from life, to fear excessively the "contamination" they might receive from the sinfulness of human affairs, to wait patiently and passively for God to accomplish his will. This does not, however, agree with the intrinsically missionary character of Christianity, which is already in evidence in the primitive Church and attested to by the New Testament literature. In our own day, both Vatican II and the meetings of the World Council of Churches have again drawn the attention of Christians to the practical task of building a world worthy of man.

Christian eschatology, like that of classic Old Testament prophetism, is a commitment to, not a flight from, the responsibilities of the present moment. Eschatology is simply another way of viewing the nature of Christianity as a community of faith, that is as a community which is constantly faced with the need to make decisions, a community which is always faced with the challenge of the Gospel to which it never adequately responds. The Christian community is never free from the divine call to deeper conversion.

Hope, decision, conversion — all of these are possible and

meaningful in the light of some vision of the future, and only in that perspective. Here again we encounter the critical importance for Christianity of the resurrection of Jesus. Sharing in it is the destiny of mankind in which Christians believe. This is the ultimate hope they cherish. All decision is measured by this goal; all conversion is motivated by it.

It is not surprising, then, that the collection of New Testament writings ends with the book of Revelations, or Apocalypse, which describes the final state of man in imaginative and revealing terms. Plainly related to the book of Ezekiel, the book of Revelations speaks of the final situation of redeemed mankind as "the heavenly Jerusalem." Gathered together in joy and peace, the people of God share with "the Lamb" the life that he has won for them by his death and resurrection. Interestingly, the image of a city is used, rather than that of a "garden of paradise." The eschatological situation, as the early Christian Church envisages it, will be one in which men will form a perfect community, sharing in the transforming experience of final union with Christ, his Father, and their Spirit.

Early Christian faith, as we find it reflected in the New Testament books, is grounded in the anticipation of unending life with the risen Christ. The Gospel it preached to men throughout the ancient world was the "good news" of life lived in freedom, the "good news" of man's liberation from sin and death. The complete realization of this hope will be achieved only when mankind has grown "to the full stature of Christ" and human history has run its course. In the meantime men can live in hope, reassured that this destiny does await them and working expectantly for its attainment, because Jesus of Nazareth, who was put to death, has risen from the dead, so that men might live.

CHAPTER FIVE

The Christ of Faith

"FAITH" CAN MEAN many things: acceptance of something as true even though one does not have direct evidence of its truth, fidelity to a personal friendship, trust in another. Even when the word is used in a religious sense, its meaning is almost as varied as the various religious situations to which it is applied. When the term "Christian faith" is used, however, the meaning is quite specific and unequivocal, at least if one is using the New Testament writings as a norm for understanding the term. Christian faith is the acceptance of the risen Christ, acceptance of the fact that he still is, that he is alive as man in fullness of human life, that he is *for* men and actively engaged in working out mankind's redemption. Most fundamentally, Christian faith is not the acceptance of a body of doctrines, nor is it the observance of laws or the performance of cult; it is a personal relationship to the risen Christ which Christians share with one another in the community of the Church.

Viewing Christian faith in this way immediately raises a critical question. If faith is this kind of personal friendship with Christ as he now is, how can a believer come into contact with him? Love and friendship cannot be directed to an abstraction; nor can they exist between two persons who have never met one another. Personal relationships require the presence of each person to the other, and this in turn is based upon genuine personal communication. It seems impossible, then, to avoid the conclusion that Christian faith must be based on some meeting between Christ and the believer, some communication between them, some presence to each other of Christ and believer.

The most authentic traditions of Christianity — beginning with those preserved in the New Testament literature and continuing down through the past two thousand years, especially in the writings of the great Christian mystics — state that such an encounter between a Christian and the risen Christ can and does take place. Without it, the centuries of Christian prayer to Christ are illusory, amounting to nothing more than an expression of men's religious needs and desires. Without it, Christianity is reduced to a group of men and women who, at best, are inspired by the teaching and example of a great man who lived two thousand years ago.

This is not to suggest that all those who have claimed for themselves the name "Christian" have possessed such a personal relationship with the risen Christ. Probably great numbers of them, even today, have had a very minimal faith or none at all. Instead, they have identified sociologically with this religious community which is the Church, but have never acquired genuine Christian faith. This should be neither surprising nor shocking, since real Christian faith is not easy to acquire or to preserve.

At the present moment in the life of the Church it is especially important that we recognize the difficulties involved in genuine Christian faith. For one reason or another, and often the reasons are complex and intertwined, faith in the risen Christ is rejected by many of our contemporaries who previously had been Christian. Even if one grants that many of these people never had genuine faith, that they had no opportunity to discover what Christianity was really all about, there are still many others who apparently had good formation in their Christian beliefs but no longer accept them. To numbers of such "unbelievers" the idea of a personal relationship to Christ sounds attractive but utterly unreal. "How can such a thing be possible?" they ask. "How can a man or woman today actually come into personal contact and relationship with the risen Christ, even if one were to grant that Christ is risen and alive?"

The question is a serious one, and it must be answered by anyone who will seriously preach the Gospel of Christ in the hope that men may believe. Nor is it an especially new question. There is abundant evidence in the New Testament writing that the early Christian communities faced the same need to explain how such personal relationship with the risen Lord was possible, since he could be neither seen nor heard nor touched. The words of John's Gospel (addressed to Thomas by the risen Christ in one of the resurrection apparitions), "Blessed are they who have not seen but have believed," must have found wide resonance among the early Christians who had not themselves witnessed immediately the life and passover of Jesus.

The Witness of the Apostles

For such converts to the Gospel the disciples of Jesus provided the witness of their own experience and faith: their experience of Jesus during the years of his public ministry, their faith in him as the risen Messiah and Lord. To bear such witness was the chief function of the Apostles (Acts 6:4); it is their witness that stands at the root of the New Testament literature. When the Church set about determining which writings should be included in the canon (the official collection) of New Testament writings, the criterion for accepting a book was its derivation from the catechesis of the Apostles.

It is interesting, then, and valuable to examine the descriptions that are given, in the Gospels and in Paul's epistles, of the first meetings of the disciples with Jesus. These descriptions are lengthy and detailed, and are apparently meant to clarify for Christian understanding the mystery of "vocation" as it applied to the followers of Christ. As

Yahweh had exercised the initiative to come in redeeming presence to his people, especially to the great prophetic figures, so now Jesus takes the initiative and calls his own disciples to follow him.

One of the earliest of these initial encounters — perhaps the very earliest — is narrated in the first chapter of John's Gospel (Jn. 1:35-41). It is instructive to note that the meeting of the two disciples with Jesus is prepared by John the Baptist's own witness to Jesus: "Behold, the Lamb of God." The two disciples of John, hearing their master's identification of Jesus as the awaited Messiah, began to follow Jesus at some distance. As he noticed them, Jesus stopped and asked, "What do you seek?" Apparently with some embarrassment they answer: "Rabbi . . . where are you staying?" To which Jesus answered in turn, "Come and see."

If, for a moment, we recall that this passage in John's Gospel was catechesis for the early Church (and has come to be such for Christian believers since that time), we can see the didactic implications of the text. The first "introduction" to Jesus as the Christ is based on the witness of others, and for the earliest followers of Jesus this witness was provided by the Baptist, whose disciples they had been. If one wished to follow Jesus, Jesus himself extended the invitation; and if one did follow him, one would "see."

The passage continues with the narration of the manner in which the two disciples who did go with Jesus and talked with him, then became in turn "witnesses" for others. Andrew, who was one of the two, came to his brother Simon (later to be known as Peter) and told him, "We have found the Messiah." In quick succession Philip and Nathanael were also invited by Jesus to join the group of his earliest disciples.

Whether or not the "vocation" of the Apostles occurred in exactly the fashion described in the Gospel texts, the fact remains that some decades later (when the Gospels were actually composed) the event of this calling was considered of some importance by the early Church. What is true of the Johannine tradition is equally true of the three Synoptic Gospels: They devote a notable amount of attention to the disciples' initial encounters with Jesus. Matthew is called from his tax-gathering to follow Jesus (Mt. 9:9); the brothers Andrew and Simon are invited to become "fishers of men" (Mt. 4:18); the two sons of Zebedee are called from their boats and nets to follow the new teacher (Mt. 4:21).

Though the details are not provided by the Gospel accounts, there must have been a similar, though perhaps less dramatic, invitation extended to many others since the circle of disciples seems to have grown quickly. Not all of these disciples, it is true, stayed with Jesus throughout his public ministry, particularly when it became increasingly evident that he was not to be the kind of Messiah that many of them anticipated and desired. But a substantial number did follow him faithfully, and these provided the nucleus of the first Christian community.

From these early followers Jesus, according to the New Testament writings, demanded very little, though, from another point of view, he demanded everything. What he asked was "faith," that is an acceptance of himself and of the message that he preached. He preached that the advent of the kingdom of God was imminent, that this was made manifest in his own ministry of preaching and healing, and that his hearers must in consequence be open to the coming of this kingdom.

To the early Christian converts who heard about Jesus of Nazareth from those who had themselves experienced him, the same challenge was presented. They, too, were called to accept Jesus in faith. Faced with this demand, they would logically have asked, and unquestionably did ask, who Jesus was and what he had done and said during the time of his earthly career. In response, the disciples of Jesus told them of their own encounter with the Master.

As they looked back on the public ministry of Jesus and their share in it, and as they reflected on those years in the light of the death and resurrection of Christ, a sense of wonder came to them, a wonder that is transmitted through the New Testament writings. The man Jesus whom they had come to know through the ordinary ways of human experience; the man with whom they had talked and eaten and worked, with whom they had shared joys and sorrows and hopes and disappointments; this man was much more than man. Man he truly was; but he was God in their midst, *Emmanuel* in the fullest sense (Mt. 1:23). He was God's own Word enfleshed and dwelling with them (Jn. 1:14). And it was this incarnated Word that they had known in personal familiarity.

> That which was from the beginning, which we have heard, which we have seen with our eyes, which we have looked upon and touched with our hands concerning the word of life — the life was made manifest, and we saw it, and testify to it, and proclaim to you the eternal life which was with the Father and was made manifest to us — that which we have seen and heard we proclaim also to you, so that you may have fellowship with us. . . .
>
> 1 Jn. 1:1-3

Realization of who this Jesus of Nazareth was transformed for the early disciples of Jesus their recollection of the experiences they shared with him. Looking back to those years when they knew him in his Galilean and Judean ministry, but looking back with the faith and insight that came through his resurrection, they understood how truly unique was the experience they had had: In ordinary human life and converse they had dealt with God's own son and word.

This experience Jesus' own disciples shared with those who, in the early decades of the Church's existence, heard the Gospel and accepted it. And they did so, not only because they wished to share what had been for them an unparalleled privilege, but because this was the supreme revelation of God to men. This was the word of life which all men needed if they were to live forever. "In many and various ways God spoke of old to our fathers by the prophets; but in these last days he has spoken to us by a Son . . ." (Heb. 1:1-2).

The writers of the New Testament literature were quite aware, then, that they were not simply recording the observable happenings of Jesus' life and death. They were transmitting, so that others might believe and be saved, the community's traditions about the revelation that had taken place in Jesus of Nazareth. It is for this reason that Christians of every succeeding historical period must search the New Testament scriptures to discover there the God who has revealed himself and who, as such, is the object of Christian faith.

In our present-day questioning about the nature and even the possibility of Christian faith, it is critically important that we examine the witness of early Christian faith which the New Testament books contain. Faith in some "God" other than the one who has revealed himself to us is meaningless, and could be nothing more than a deceptive illustration, an anthropomorphic projection of our desires or needs or fears. Religiously, such false "faith" would constitute a deep-seated form of idolatry that would be a barrier to belief in the true God. And to search for justification of such false belief would be an utter waste of time and energy.

If one is to examine Christian faith — and such critical examination is for many a necessary stepping-stone to mature faith — then one must deal with what that faith really is: the personal acceptance in community of the God who reveals himself in Jesus, who is the word incarnate. Such examination may lead a person either to accept or to reject the faith of Christianity. But both acceptance and rejection, if they are to be honest, must deal with the authentic Gospel of Christianity and not with some caricature of it.

Self-revelation of the Word

To return to the New Testament writings, what is the revelation of God about which they speak? Clearly, it is the revelation that has taken place in Christ, particularly in the culminating event of his death and resurrection. The content of his teaching, the significance of his actions, the relationship he bears to the revealing events of Old Testament history, all form part of this revelation. But most basically, it is Jesus himself who is the revelation: What he reveals is himself. This he does through his words and deeds, and supremely in his total gift of self through death and resurrection. His act of revelation is an act of self-revelation, and this is why he can identify faith with acceptance of himself.

The early Church's belief that Jesus of Nazareth is the revelation of God is inseparable from its belief that he is the Word. Those among the early Christians who were Jewish — and at the very beginning this was the majority — would have been familiar with the Old Testament notion of "the word of Yahweh." From the opening portion of the book of Genesis they would have been accustomed to think that Yahweh created the world by the power of his word. Again, the prophetic books that they would have heard again and again in the synagogue service spoke repeatedly about the word of Yahweh, the word that he placed in the mouth of the prophet, a word that was filled with power, a word through which life was meant to come to men.

Jesus himself, when he appeared publicly to teach and begin the work of establishing his Father's kingdom, was looked upon as a prophet who had been sent by God. His words were considered, at least by some of his hearers, as being words of power: "This man speaks with authority. . . ." Moreover, the Gospel texts tell us that the words of Jesus had power to work wonders: To the widow's son at Naim he *said,* "Young man, I say to you, arise," and the young man came back to life (Lk. 7:14). By simply speaking he cured the blind and the crippled. His words were clearly a source of life and of healing.

After the resurrection the disciples of Jesus began to realize the full dimension of his prophetic possession of God's word. He was not just the greatest of the prophets, he was himself the Father's word incarnated. The Father had so loved men that he had sent his own son, his own word, to tell men that they were the object of divine love and were therefore destined for unending life and joy. The one condition that men would have to fulfill in order to have this life was to believe, to accept this Word who was sent to them.

This meant that in Jesus the early disciples had not only encountered the word of God, they had also encountered the Father. It is the function of a word to make the hearer aware not just of the word that is spoken but also of the one who speaks. The Father had spoken to men in his word so that men might know him as the Father, trust in him, and come to freedom and life.

It is evident that during the public life of Jesus his disciples were not aware of this contact with the Father which Jesus as word provided for them. They heard Jesus talking incessantly about his Father, about the kingdom of his Father, about his Father's love and care for men; but they did not realize how immediately the Father was manifested to them in Jesus. John's Gospel tells us about the incident at the Last Supper when Philip, one of the twelve who was at table with Jesus, turned to Jesus and asked him when he would show them the Father (Jn. 14:5-11). Jesus' answer touches the very depths of the incarnation: "He who has seen me, has seen the Father." Because he was the Son spoken humanly to men, Jesus' very being revealed his Father.

One cannot pretend to grasp adequately this mystery of the Father's self-revelation in Jesus, but reflection on a somewhat parallel human situation may give us some understanding. Suppose there is a child of nine or ten years, with whom I have been working as a teacher and counselor closely for many months, with whom I have an excellent relationship that allows me to know this child quite thoroughly and accurately. I have come to know the child's ideas and dreams, his fears and worries, his security and insecurity, his ambitions and personal secrets. Suppose, too, that I have never had occasion to meet the child's father. Yet from knowing this child I have a very good knowledge of the father. I do not know how good a business man or craftsman he is, I do not know how effective he is in public life; I do not know his hobbies or skills or athletic interests; but I do know what kind of a father he is, for this is reflected in the influence he has had on his child.

In the human situation, this means that I know only one aspect of the personality of the child's father, for this man is many things, one of which is to be father to this child. With God the Father, the situation is different. Being the Father of this son who is incarnated in Jesus of Nazareth is the totality of the Father's personhood. This is exactly what makes him to be the person he is. Thus, in knowing his son, Jesus, and seeing what his Father means to him and has done for him, one should be able to know the Father himself.

This illustrates the importance of discovering just exactly who Jesus of Nazareth is. If he is to function as the sign, the word, of his Father, he himself must be recognized as the Son and as the Word. And if we can judge from the experience of the early disciples of Jesus, it takes some time to discover Jesus' true identity. It is simple enough for a Christian today to repeat the statement that Jesus is the son of God the Father, that he is the incarnate word. It is quite another thing to discover what this means and to discover that it is really true.

When Jesus first began to teach and attract followers to himself, these disciples had no inkling of the divine identity of this man. They looked on him as a magnetic human being, as a man whom they admired and with whom they wished to be associated, as a teacher who made more sense to them than did the official religious teachers of their day. Such teachers were not uncommon at that time. John the Baptist had himself attracted such a group of devoted disciples.

It seems that before too long Jesus of Nazareth was looked upon as more than just another teacher; he was truly a prophet, perhaps even the great prophet that many of the Jews were expecting. In the Gospels Jesus is clearly depicted as this great prophet. His message and his deeds are explicitly compared with the message and deeds of the great Old Testament prophets (Lk. 7:11-17; 1 Kings 17:17); he is not only the continuation but the fulfillment of that great prophetic tradition (Mt. 21:33-46). It is less clear how much of this unique prophetic stature was recognized by Jesus' disciples during the years of his public ministry, but there is little doubt that they came to view him as a true prophet.

Somewhat longer was the process of discovering that Jesus was the long-awaited Messiah. From all the indications of the Gospels, it was well along into the public life of Jesus before even his closest followers recognized him as the Messiah — and most of the people never did see him as such. Part of the problem seems to have been rooted in Jesus' own reluctance to be acclaimed as Messiah. Such reluctance is mentioned in the Gospel narratives, and if it actually was Jesus' attitude on the subject it can probably be explained by the numerous misunderstandings of the coming Messiah that the people cherished. Many, for example, were anticipating a militant leader who would lead them in bloody and triumphant rebellion against their Roman overlords. To have fostered such violent hopes would have been dangerous and misleading.

To his immediate followers, however, the insight gradually came that Jesus was indeed the Messiah. According to the

Gospels, this realization was awakened by the multiplica-
tion of the loaves which Jesus had given as a sign of his role
(Mt. 14:15-21). Apparently, most of the people had missed
the significance of this action, and Jesus queries his disciples:
"Who do you say that I am?" To which Simon Peter replies,
"You are the Christ [the Messiah], the Son of the living
God" (Mt. 16:16).

But this was only half the insight. Jesus was Messiah,
but what kind of Messiah? His disciples seemed to share
many elements of the popular expectations. Even if Jesus
was not planning to instigate a revolution, he did seem to
be thinking about some future kingdom in which he would
reign; and in such a kingdom they would logically find places
of honor. If one reads between the lines in the Gospel accounts, it appears that the disciples cherished quite a ma-
terialistic vision of the coming kingdom and its rewards.
The death of Jesus was required to destroy this false pre-
supposition.

Jesus himself tried to disabuse his disciples of the mistaken meaning they were still attaching to his messianic
identity and role. He was Messiah indeed, but Messiah
according to the pattern of the Servant described in the
fifty-second chapter of Isaiah, one who by his suffering and
rejection brings salvation for his people. With increasing
clarity and frequency he spoke of the need to go down to
Jerusalem, so that there he might be put to death (Mt.
16:21).

In all fairness to the disciples of Jesus, it must be admitted
that such a prediction must have seemed paradoxical at best.
As Simon Peter pointed out to Jesus, this was no way to go
about the business of being the Messiah (Mt. 16:22). Nor
did it help that Jesus, when he spoke of his coming death,
added "and rise again." To us, looking back to the public
life of Jesus with our knowledge of his resurrection, the
statement "The Son of man must go down to Jerusalem, to
suffer and die, and then rise again" seems quite straight-

forward and understandable. But we must remember that
Jesus was the first man to go from death to resurrection.
This had never occurred before, was not something the
disciples were in any way expecting (as their reaction to
the resurrection indicates), and so did not make any great
impact on their understanding.

It is quite probable that the disciples heard Jesus speak
of the suffering and death he would have to undergo shortly,
but would not let themselves accept these predictions as realistic. With the events of Holy Week, however, all this was
changed. Suddenly, all the hopes and dreams of glory that
the band of disciples had cherished were shattered by Jesus'
apprehension, trial, and death. He whom they had hoped
was the expected Messiah of Israel died the shameful death
of a criminal, crucifixion on the hill of Calvary outside the
city (Lk. 24:19-20).

Though his followers did not realize it at the time – they
were hardly in the mood for theological reflection – the
suffering and death of Jesus were his culminating prophetic
message, his fulfillment of the Old Testament prophetic
passages that spoke of the Servant and of the salvific power
of his afflictions, and his key witness to the Father in whom
he trusted. Enigmatic though the statement may appear, it
is literally true to say that the death of Jesus was the greatest
act of his life on this earth, his greatest revelation to men of
his own and his Father's love for them.

After the Resurrection

With Jesus' death, the normal means by which men could
encounter him are obviously no longer operative. While he
lived, men could see and hear him, speak with him, enjoy
his company at meals; but all this ceased with Calvary.
From this point onward the question of Christian faith becomes real and pressing: If one does believe in Christ, does
believe that he passed through death into a new life that
we call "resurrection," and does wish to relate personally

to this Christ, how does he go about contacting Christ? Death, even the death of Jesus, seems to close all the doors to communication with those who have died.

Yet, however one wishes to explain it (or to explain it away), the New Testament writings state explicitly that personal contact with Jesus did not cease with his death. The Gospels all contain descriptions of the appearances — at least some of them — that the risen Christ made to his disciples after his death. Such appearances occurred for only a short time, perhaps to reassure the disciples that Jesus was still with them, though now in risen form.

There is no way of knowing exactly in what these post-Easter apparitions of Christ consisted. The accounts in the Gospels are brief and without detailed descriptions of Jesus in his risen state. The Gospels, after all, were not written to give us an analytic explanation of risen life as possessed by the risen Christ, but to provide a witness to the fact that he was risen, so that others might believe also. Besides, as one reads and rereads the accounts of the post-Easter appearances, he gets the impression that these apparitions of Jesus in his risen state, though they were real, were mysterious and puzzling to the disciples. Such apparitions are hardly a normal part of a human being's experience! It must have taken some time for the disciples to become accustomed to the idea that Jesus was really alive.

Despite, then, a certain vagueness in the Gospel accounts of the appearances of the risen Christ, some things emerge as definite in the early Church's faith about the resurrection. First, and most important, it had happened. Jesus had really passed through the experience of death into that of new and risen life. Whatever theoretical problems or questions one might raise about the possibilities of such a thing, the disciples of Jesus were firm in their conviction that Jesus was risen, for they had seen him and conversed with him in those days after Easter. This experience was their impetus to preach the Gospel of resurrection; it also gave them their credentials to do so (Acts 5:32).

Secondly, though unquestionably he was different than he had been in the days before his death and resurrection, the risen Christ was the same Jesus the disciples had known. Though it seems that they did not immediately recognize him — and there is no indication of exactly why this was so — they very shortly discovered that it was he. The Gospel accounts tell us that Jesus himself was at pains to let them know that it was truly he: "Why are you troubled . . . ? . . . it is I myself" (Lk. 24:38, 39). There is no doubt in the minds of the Christians who produced the New Testament literature, because there was no doubt in the minds of the early disciples whose witness is the foundation for that literature, that the risen Christ who appeared in the days after Easter was the same Jesus who had lived and worked among them in Galilee and Judea.

Thirdly, the risen Christ remains with his disciples. His resurrection and ascension are not a mystery of departure from human life and human history, but a mystery of *presence*. According to the account in Luke's Gospel, the last words of Jesus before he terminated his final apparition were, "I am with you always, to the close of the age" (Mt. 28:20). What the ascension of Christ means is his passage into a manner of being human which is not commensurate with our present experience of space and time. Because of this incommensurability we are unable to experience him through our senses. Moreover, the Gospel scene of the ascension is meant to teach the fact that the risen Jesus has passed to full possession of the Spirit, to full participation in the glory of his Father. None of this indicates an absence of the risen Christ from those who are his disciples.

Finally, there is some connection between the resurrection-appearances of Jesus and his special presence to Christians when they join together for the eucharistic celebration. Modern scholarship has not yet studied this connection carefully enough for us to make firm judgments about it. However, it is quite striking, once one's attention is drawn to the fact, that almost all the apparitions described in the Gospels occur in conjunction with a meal: the two appearances to the disciples in the same upper room where the Last Supper had been held (Jn. 20); the appearance to the two disciples on their way to Emmaus, in which they recognize him "in the breaking of the bread" (Lk. 24:31); the appearance on the shores of the Sea of Galilee when Jesus prepares breakfast for the disciples (Jn. 20:21). These apparitions of the risen Christ may be narrated in the Gospels for the catechetical purpose of assuring the early Christians that the risen Lord himself was present to them when they gathered for the eucharistic "breaking of the bread."

To the points we have just mentioned another might be added, if for no other reason than the fact that many Christians today do not seem to be too clear about it, namely that the risen Christ who is described in the Gospels is a man. He has passed into a new life, one which is apparently freed from many of this earthly life's limitations, but this new life is human life. Jesus is still humanly conscious; his consciousness obviously is the continuation of the one he had before his death, for he speaks to his disciples about the experiences they had shared in those early days. The fact that he appears to his friends and assures them of his friendship despite their abandonment of him during his passion makes it clear that he still possesses a human affectivity that continues the human affection he had before his death. And even though his bodily existence is clearly other than that which he formerly had, the risen Christ still exists in some bodily form.

For the early disciples of Jesus there were two levels of personal encounter with him. During his earthly life they had been able to know him and deal with him as they did with any other man of their day; in the days following his resurrection they encountered this same Jesus, but now in his risen glory. Because of this unique experience these disciples became the witnesses whose testimony grounds the faith of all succeeding generations of Christians.

One of the most influential of these early witnesses enjoyed only the second of the two types of immediate encounter with Christ that we have just described. This was Saul of Tarsus, whom history knows as St. Paul. He certainly was not among the disciples who followed Jesus in his public life. Most likely he never had any direct contact with Jesus prior to his death and resurrection, and he began as a fanatical opponent to the early Christians. His meeting with Christ came in that famous occurrence on the road from Jerusalem to Damascus when, blinded by the light from on high, he fell to the ground and heard the voice of the risen Jesus, "Saul, why do you persecute me?" (Acts 9:14).

Though Paul tells the Galatians that he was privileged with other revelations of Christ (Gal. 1:15-17), this first experience of the risen Jesus remained for Paul the governing experience of his life. Three years later he would have the opportunity to confer with Peter and James in Jerusalem, and again, fourteen years later, to meet with the Apostles who were still in Jerusalem (Gal. 1:18; 2:1). But these meetings did not provide him with his fundamental understanding of the risen Christ or of Christian life; this came from his own experience of Jesus, who as the risen Lord had revealed himself to him. For this reason Paul stands with the twelve Apostles as a privileged witness to the resurrection of Christ.

There is a marked difference in emphasis between the Gospels and the letters of Paul when they speak about Christ. In Paul there is relatively little attention paid to the earthly life of Jesus. Not that he is unaware of Jesus' public ministry of teaching and healing, or disinterested in it. But by the time that Paul came to know Jesus, it was already the era of the Church. The death and resurrection of Christ had occurred, and it was in this context of the full manifestation of Christ that Paul encountered him. The Jesus whom Paul met for the first time was the risen Lord. This meeting was the beginning of Paul's own faith-history, and it is within this framework that he thinks and speaks of Christ.

One of the most notable aspects of Paul's view of Christ is his constant stress on the presence of the risen Christ to Christians. This awareness of Christ's relationship to the Church is probably rooted in Paul's own conversion experience. When he had been blinded by the light and thrown to the ground on the way to Damascus, the voice had asked him: "Saul, Saul, why do you persecute *me?*" And when Paul had said "Who are you, Lord?" the answer came back, "I am Jesus, whom you are persecuting." Obviously the action of persecution referred to is that of Saul against the early followers of Jesus. Yet the risen Christ so identifies with these followers that he speaks of the persecution as something done against himself.

This passage which describes Saul's encounter with the risen Christ so succinctly (it is recounted four times — Acts 9:3-8; 22:4-16; 26:9-18; Gal. 1:13-17 — but the variant accounts add little by way of detail), provides at least three valuable elements for our insight into early Christian faith in Christ. First of all, it is clear from this event that in his risen state Christ is humanly conscious of what is happening in the lives of his followers. Behind his accusation against Saul lies his knowledge that such a persecution of the Jerusalem Christians had been pursued by Saul and his allies. And it is worth noting that he identifies himself to Saul by his proper name as a man. He does not use a title like Christ or Lord, but says, "I am Jesus. . . ."

Paul's experience supports the point we made earlier in discussing the Gospel accounts of the post-Easter apparitions: Resurrection and ascension are not a matter of Christ's departure from his disciples but rather a mystery of his enduring presence to them. Paul's experience surely indicates that the risen Jesus had been close to his followers, aware of the difficulties they were encountering, and watching over them to guide and protect them.

Another point which this passage indicates is the assurances possessed by the early Christians that they could contact the risen Christ. If one thing seems clear from this account it is that Paul felt (then and later) that the risen Christ had actually spoken to him and that he (Paul) had actually spoken to Christ. Nor does the account in Acts 9 see this occurrence as a totally unique thing, for the passage goes on to tell how Christ then appeared to Ananias in Damascus, preparing him to receive Saul and baptize him. Without trying to give any analysis or explanation of the various "visions" of Christ about which the Acts of the Apostles and Paul's epistles speak, we can at the moment notice the mentality of faith that is here involved: The risen Jesus is not only watchful over his Church, guiding and protecting it by the power of his Spirit, but he is in constant contact with it and open to the prayers addressed to him by his followers. For the early Christians, communication with the risen Christ was not a theoretical possibility; it was a fact of experience.

Still another facet of early Christian faith is contained in the passage we are discussing: the risen Christ's profound identification with Christians. In some of his letters, such as those to the Corinthians, Paul will speak about the Christian community as "the body of Christ," indicating thereby the intimacy and immediacy of the relation between Christ and his Church. It is not hard to see the connection between this teaching of Paul and his own initial experience of the risen Christ — "Saul, why do you persecute me?" From the very beginning of his life of faith in Christ, Paul had known the risen Lord precisely as related to the infant Christian community.

Two stages of immediate and sensible encounter with Jesus of Nazareth are, then, the origin of the early Church:

the experience his disciples had had of him prior to his resurrection; the experiences that these same disciples and
Paul had of him as the risen Lord. One cannot speak of
these two types of encounter as "sensible" in exactly the
same way, but it is difficult to find any other word to
describe the character of the post-Easter experiences.

Faith and Community

But what of those converts to Christianity who had neither
known Jesus in his earthly life and ministry nor been privileged with the apparition of the risen Jesus after Easter?
For them faith had to be a process of believing without
themselves seeing Christ. Here we find the problem of
Christian faith as we know it today: How can we somehow
come into contact with the risen Christ? How can we establish the kind of personal relationship with him that the New
Testament writings describe as "faith"? How can we know
that he really *is* now, and that he is for us?

There are a number of passages in the New Testament
literature that suggest these very questions were already
being posed by converts in the first century of the Church's
life. One such passage is in John's Gospel and describes the
second appearance of the risen Jesus to the disciples in the
upper room (Jn. 20:26-29). Thomas, one of the Twelve
who had been missing a week earlier when Jesus had appeared in the group, and who had been skeptical about the
reality of the resurrection, professes his faith when he
actually sees Jesus. The risen Christ then says to Thomas —
and one can feel the catechetical implications for the early
Christians who would read the Gospel or hear it — "Because
you have seen you have believed; blessed are they who have
not seen but have believed."

This would seem to indicate that faith, specifically Christian faith in the risen Christ and in his Father who sends
him as mankind's redeemer, is an acceptance of what one
does not see. Actually, the epistle to the Hebrews describes

faith this way: "Faith is the assurance of things hoped for, the conviction of things not seen" (Heb. 11:1). One must admit honestly that this definition of Christian faith raises many questions for one who is a Christian or is thinking of becoming one. Certainly, it is not a mature or praiseworthy action if a person accepts in complete blind assent something as ultimate as the Gospel; on the other hand, what basis can a person have for accepting the resurrection and continuing presence of Christ?

Not only the content, but the very existence of the New Testament books, provides us with part of the answer to such a query, or at least the answer the early Christians gave to it. To their way of thinking, faith in the risen Christ is justified because of the *witness* of those who had more immediately experienced him in his life and particularly in his resurrection. When the Apostles went out to proclaim the Gospel, this was their "proof" for the reality of that which they announced: We have ourselves seen it. This, too, was why the Church preserved those writings that comprise the New Testament: They contain the traditional witness of Jesus' own disciples.

For all later generations of Christian believers the testimony of the disciples who actually experienced Jesus' death and resurrection is an indispensable foundation for faith in Christ. On the basis of this "historical evidence" one can construct a carefully reasoned argument for the validity of Christian faith, pointing out that there is no reason for doubting the credibility of the early Christian witnesses to Christ, showing how that witness was carefully and objectively recorded, and so forth. Such argumentation has been painstakingly developed, especially in the so-called "apologetics" that marked so much of the nineteenth and early twentieth century justification for Christian faith. And certainly such examination of the historical witness to the reality of Christ's resurrection is of great value in solidifying a present-day Christian's conviction about the death and resurrection of Jesus as real happenings.

By itself, however, such a line of argumentation does not provide all that is needed for true Christian faith. As we have seen, the books of the New Testament make it evident that faith is not just a theoretical assent to the fact that something happened; it is a personal acceptance of and relationship to a particular person, the risen Jesus. This seems to mean that the Christian believer must somehow himself come into contact with the risen Christ, must somehow have an experiential awareness of Christ's present reality. In other words, we have come back to the question with which we began this chapter: How does a Christian encounter the living and risen Christ today?

The essential element in answering this question is the faith-witness of others, though now we must stress the witness of Christians today rather than that of the Christians of Jesus' own day. Valuable and indispensable as the early Christian witness is, the starting-point for a Christian's faith today, the most fundamental piece of evidence from which he works in realizing the present reality of Christ, is the faith-witness of his fellow Christians. Because he has known and still knows men and women who believe in the risen Christ, men and women he knows and trusts and who have made their own faith in Christ apparent to him, a person today can have faith in Christ.

This is not the only basis for faith, as we will see. Christian faith is a gift from God; it depends upon that continuing self-revelation of Christ and of his Father to which faith is a response. But this divine action takes place in conjunction with faith-witness of the Christian community. Paul mentions this fact in his letter to the Romans (10:14-15, 17): "... how are they to believe in him of whom they have never heard? And how are they to hear without a preacher? ... So faith comes from what is heard, and what is heard comes by the preaching of Christ."

Still, the question persists: How can this actually happen? How can the faith of my fellow Christians create in me a consciousness of the reality of the risen Christ, a consciousness of his presence in the world today? Reflection on one or two common human situations may help to throw light on the situation of Christian faith.

Take, for our first example, the case of a child growing up in a home where he hears regular references to his Uncle John. This uncle has been off in a foreign country for years, with the result that the child has never had any immediate experience of him. Yet the child has an unquestioning conviction of this man's reality. Why? Because of the witness of his parents to the uncle's existence and characteristics and activities. They make no point at all of trying to prove the uncle's existence to the child, but the very way in which they speak of "Uncle John" makes it perfectly clear that they themselves are convinced of his reality.

Similar to this is the context in which the faith of many, perhaps most, Christians has come into existence. Born into a thoroughly Christian home, where the parents truly believed in the reality and importance of Christ, the child grew up under constant exposure to the faith-witness of his parents. The parents' manner of talking about Christ, about God the Father, were so matter-of-factly realistic and convincing that the realities of faith were almost taken for granted by the growing child. In the early years of life, when faith was gradually coming into existence in the child's consciousness, it was principally the faith of his parents that served as the criterion for belief. If the person is fortunate, this early home witness to Christ's reality is followed by exposure to the living faith of teachers, friends, or other associates, all of which helps to solidify the person's own faith.

Another example may help to make a somewhat different point. During a national political convention one can find, in almost any town or city, small, enthusiastic groups of dedicated people who give their time and energy to the campaign of their favorite candidate. Many of these people have never met the candidate for whom they are working, but they do know others who have met him, dealt with him, discussed electoral issues with him, and caught some of his viewpoint and spirit. And through such "lucky" ones who have actually had the good fortune to know the candidate personally, the others come to think of the candidate as someone they themselves know, to whose cause they are devoted, whose ideas they share. One thing that never enters the mind of these campaign workers is to question the actual reality of the man to whose election they are committed. On the contrary, everything around them would be unmeaning nonsense if the candidate were only the figment of someone's imagination.

Admittedly, the parallel between this situation and that of a Christian in the Church is not a perfect one. Yet there are many groups of thoroughly dedicated Christians who work together to carry on in the world the task of human betterment, and who do so because of their relationship to Christ. To experience the enthusiasm and generosity of these people, to be exposed to their firm conviction of the reality and importance of Christ, would surely strengthen the Christian faith of one who wished to believe. Unfortunately, a large number of men who think of themselves as Christian have never had the opportunity to experience such a vital Christian community.

This lack in the lives of many Christians may help to explain the relatively low level of faith they possess — and it may point to the need to do something about this situation. It does not seem that Christian faith can develop and flourish without the support of a community of believers; nor could faith even come into existence if such a community were totally lacking.

Each Christian is dependent upon the faith of his fellow Christians as a norm and criterion of his own acceptance of

Christ. Even his own idea of who Christ was and is, of what Christ did and does, comes to him through the teaching he has received, the conversations he has had, the sermons he has heard, the books he has read. Dependent upon such sources, a person's understanding of Christ is more or less accurate. Equally, if not more, important is his dependence upon other believers for his knowledge of the fact that Christ is — not just that he was, but that he now is the risen Lord.

For most Christians, their life of faith came into being within the believing community of their own family. In a daily and unsystematic fashion, the parents shared with their children a conviction about the reality and importance of Christ; and without being given any specific arguments about the claims of Christ to be the son of God become man or about the claims of the Church to be the guardian of the Gospel, the children in such a family developed their own sense of the existence of Christ and his Father. As they grew into adulthood — if they were fortunate — the faith of their childhood was reinforced by the friends and teachers who also shared with them their Christian faith.

If one is to be honest, he must admit that the process we have just sketched did not occur in the lives of very many people who think of themselves as "Catholic," but whose understanding and acceptance of the risen Christ is minimal or almost non-existent. There are within the vast sociological reality of the Church, within the hundreds of millions who "belong to the Church," a fairly large number who must still be converted to genuine Christian faith in the risen Christ and in his Father. In great part this is true because these men and women have never in their life had the experience of a community of Christians who truly believed, a community whose faith they themselves could begin to share.

At the risk of being repetitive, it is important to emphasize the fact that such a community provides more than information about the Church and its doctrines and practices; it provides more even than the "argument" for Chris-

THE CHRIST OF FAITH   165

tianity that comes in seeing intelligent and mature people accepting the truth of Christ and the Church. In an intangible but real way, such a community of believers provides the opportunity for a person to encounter the continuing reality of the risen Christ and of his Spirit. Such an "encounter" with Christ need not be, and for the most part is not, a sharply experienced consciousness of Christ's presence. Instead, it is a quietly developing element of a believer's awareness of himself and of his life experience. Though such an experience is faith and always remains faith, and is therefore quite different from the kind of knowing attached to direct sensible experience, the believer's developing awareness of Christ and of his action in his life is truly a form of knowledge. But it is a knowledge that can be possessed only by sharing faith with other believers.

Critically important and indispensable though it be, the community of faith in which the believer shares is not the only criterion and basis for his faith. As his faith comes into being it necessarily involves a growing personal relationship to Christ, for that is what faith is. A Christian accepts Christ along with his fellow Christians, he accepts Christ in dependence upon the witness of their faith. But it is Christ whom he, an individual believer, accepts in faith. Though shared with others, the believing Christian's relationship with Christ is *his,* and is, to that extent, unique and distinctive.

As this experience of Christ in faith develops as part of a Christian's consciousness, it provides its own criterion for the reality of Christ. The believer knows Christ — which is quite different than knowing about Christ — and this kind of knowing would be impossible if the risen Christ were not real.

At this point, it might seem that we are talking about a rare phenomenon in Christian experience, the kind of unusual consciousness that one associates with the great mystics. Authentic Christian mystics (men and women like Teresa of Avila or John of the Cross or Ignatius Loyola) did possess in special intensity an awareness of the reality and presence of the risen Christ. But theirs was still an awareness in faith, and a lesser degree of the same awareness belongs to each Christian who directs his love and prayer to Christ and in doing so has the experience of "talking to someone."

Prayer and Liturgy

What this means is that prayer, in some form or other, is a necessary part of a Christian's life of faith. This prayer can take many expressions, many forms; it need not be formalized or structured or spoken in "prayers," though some of this is often helpful. Essentially it is a directing of one's attention, one's consciousness and one's affection to Christ (or to the Father). As such, it is a process of communication, mysterious but real. This kind of personal contact with Christ, whose reality can be accepted and experienced only in faith, has been part of the lives of countless millions of Christians over the past two thousand years.

In a sense, the encounter of the believer with Christ that takes place in prayer begins where the witness of the Christian community stops. The community witness provides the starting point, an always necessary starting point, for the Christian's realization of the living presence of Christ. But upon that foundation the Christian goes on to his own personal relationship to the risen Lord, a relationship he can then share with his fellow Christians and in this way be a support to their faith. Neither the faith of the individual Christian nor the shared faith of the community can exist apart from each other.

During the past decade or two, we have become increasingly aware of the role of the community in the life of Christian faith. This is a great gain. For too long our approach to Christianity was excessively individualistic. At the same time, there is some danger that in the enthusiasm and gratification of experiencing such Christian community, people will make that community itself the total object of their awareness, as if the acceptance of one another in community is the acceptance of Christ. These two are certainly intertwined; it is not possible to accept Christ and refuse the community.

But the community does not replace Christ; in fact, it becomes a Christian community only by its corporate acceptance of the risen Christ. Deep as their devotion was to one another, the early Christians whose experience of community is reflected in the pages of the New Testament were not united primarily by that devotion, but by their faith in the risen Christ.

There was one privileged situation in which the early Christians were able to share their faith with one another and communally give expression to it: the gathering of the community for the "breaking of bread," the eucharistic celebration of Jesus' death and resurrection. This, too, was the occasion when each Christian and the community as a whole were able to experience the abiding presence of the risen Lord. "Where two or three are gathered together in my name, there I am in the midst of them" (Mt. 18:20).

So, too, for Christians today, the community celebration of the Eucharist is meant to be the foremost occasion for encountering the Christ in whom they believe. Against the truth of this statement an objection is often raised: In actuality, this does not seem to happen; even well-intentioned and interested Christians find their experience of the Eucharist anything but a shared awareness of the redeeming presence of the risen Lord. If this is true — and, sadly, it seems to be the case for the great majority of people — it only points to the obvious need of completing the task of liturgical reform that is demanded by Vatican II's Decree on the Liturgy. Any such reform, as the Council's decree insists, must be guided by the objective of creating a eucharistic action that is truly an experienced sharing of faith.

Such revitalization of the eucharistic liturgy is already well under way in the present-day Church, although, as always happens in social change, there is a marked advance in some groups and a noticeable lag in others. The impetus given liturgical revival by Vatican II is a solid source of hope for the future. Equally hopeful is a deepened understanding of the Eucharist, an understanding that is no longer confined to theological experts but is seeping into the awareness of large masses of the faithful. As understanding of the nature of the eucharistic action becomes more accurate, the experience of celebrating the Eucharist will change accordingly, forcing an alteration of liturgical forms so they will agree with the intrinsic reality of this experience.

For the question we are discussing in this chapter — the manner in which Christians can come into contact with Christ and accept him in faith — it is vitally necessary that the Eucharist be understood, and concretely experienced, as an action in which the community professes its faith in the risen Christ who is present in their midst. Each Christian as he participates in the Eucharist is meant to find support for his own faith in the faith of his brethren and to support them by his faith. As each acknowledges publicly and explicitly his belief in the risen Christ, this is a witness to all those present, a proclamation of the Gospel. For children the Eucharist should be an extension of the faith-witness that they have in the home; for adults it should be the continuation and intensification of the various human groupings in which they are exposed to the Christian faith of others.

This does not mean that the celebration of the Eucharist is always the most acute experience one has of his Christian faith. It may well be that from time to time a Christian will undergo some experience that will make him sharply aware of what it means to be Christian. He may meet a person whose faith radiates a sense of the reality of Christ; or he may share with some fellow Christians an involvement in a critically important social action; or he may witness the death of one who dies with obvious Christian trust in the resurrection. Hopefully, some celebrations of the Eucharist will be marked by a realization in some depth of the mystery of Christ. More important is the steadily developing clarification and intensification of faith that takes place almost imperceptibly in one's life.

This gradual development of the life of faith among Christians should be a response to the word of God that is spoken to those who share in the Eucharist. Not only the early portion of the Mass, in which the text of Scripture is used, but the entire action of the Eucharist is a "liturgy of the word." What the texts from the Bible are talking about, the action of the Eucharist is making present and effective: the continuing mystery of Christ's death and resurrection. And it is in and through the risen Christ, himself present in the Eucharist to the assembled faithful, that God the Father reveals himself to his people and thereby makes it possible for them to encounter him in faith.

The Eucharist is a special situation for encountering Christ and his Father, because it effects a more intensive presence of Christ to the Christian community. The risen Christ is always present to those who accept him in faith, but the eucharistic action is a heightening of that presence precisely because it is an action of personal communication; it is God's word to men and their response of faith. This presupposes, of course, some consciousness on the part of those celebrating the Eucharist, some awareness of the significance of the act they are doing. To arouse such consciousness, to allow the Eucharist to function effectively as a "word," is a primary objective of the liturgical ceremonies of the Mass.

Personal presence is established through communication by one person to another; the deeper the level of self-giving involved in this communication, the deeper is the level of presence. Since the Eucharist is the continuing of Christ's death and resurrection, his supreme act of self-giving, it is intrinsically the situation of unique presence between Christ and Christians. Other things being equal, it is first and foremost in the eucharistic action that Christians, individually and corporately, should be able to come into personal contact with the risen Christ.

Catholic theology and catechetics have often expressed the result of this eucharistic encounter by saying that Christians "receive grace" as a result of it. This means, among other things, that those who share in the eucharistic action are changed as a result, that they are affected by the divine influence. If change is brought about through eucharistic participation, it certainly must occur primarily in the sphere of faith, in the understandings men have of themselves in relationship to God. This is exactly what the encounter with the risen Christ is meant to accomplish; it is intended to be a radical challenge to our ideas of the divine, of salvation, and of sanctity. As the New Testament literature insists repeatedly, the risen Christ (and therefore Christianity) is a *new being;* in him religion takes on a *new meaning;* through his death and resurrection human life and human history take on a *new purpose.*

The Challenge of Encounter

Personal encounter in faith with the risen Christ is a radical challenge to mankind's understanding of the divine, because Christ is the divine expressed humanly. The reality of incarnation, Jesus as the Word become man, wipes out any notion of a God who is aloof and distant from men and their needs and experiences. Jesus, as the New Testament writers describe him, is Emmanuel, God-with-us, the sacrament of his Father's presence to men. The awesome implication of the incarnation is that God wishes to enter into immediate and intimate relationship with men. In this instance the law of love and friendship — the law that the one loving seeks identification with the person he loves — finds expression in the Son's identification with men to the extent of becoming man.

THE CHRIST OF FAITH   171

Paradoxically, however, the intimacy of God's real presence to men does not deny his transcendance; it actually intensifies and safeguards it. "The transcendance of God" means that God is not his creation; that he is clearly distinct from it. As the New Testament writings (and for that matter, the Old Testament writings in their own way) treat the transcendance of God, the distinction between him and men is recognized as that between creator and creatures; but this is not what is emphasized. What is stressed is the irreducible "otherness" of God the Father as the "other person" to whom men are related in love.

If I have a friend to whom I relate in love, it is clear that I am not he. Though the friendship does tend towards a deepening identification and unity between my friend and myself, it also leads (if it is a mature relationship) to a deepening respect for the other person's distinctiveness. So, too, the deepening of a relationship between a believer and God the Father (or Christ) causes a more intense respect for the distinctiveness of the Father. This is a preservative against idolatry, for the believer avoids making God over "according to man's image and likeness." Instead, he opens himself to the need of changing his understanding of the divine, in order to conform to what God really is.

We might add that such an openness to the otherness of God the Father is difficult and even frightening. The reality of God, when it is actually encountered in the experience of faith, challenges not only our religious understandings, but also our understandings of everything else. Fortunately, this challenge takes place in the context of the Father's love for men; it is this love that provides the security needed by men to face the risk involved.

There may be, then, a certain threat connected with a Christian's encounter with Christ and the Father. This is utterly different, however, from the notion of a threatening and angry God. Jesus' parables, like the one in which he describes the father of the prodigal son, are a direct attack upon the idea of a wrathful and menacing God. There is a relentlessness that characterizes the Father's attitude toward men; there is an implacable hostility of the Father towards evil; but (as the New Testament describes it) this means that God's love constantly seeks out man to save him, and that this love cannot countenance the evil that would destroy man. All the New Testament traditions stress God's search for the sinner in order to win him back.

Again, the New Testament writings do not deny the Old Testament belief that God has revealed himself as the law-giver. Indeed, Matthew's Gospel records the saying of Jesus: "Think not that I have come to abolish the law and the prophets; I have come not to abolish them but to fulfill them. For truly, I say to you, till heaven and earth pass away, not an iota not a dot, will pass from the law until all is accomplished" (Mt. 5:17-18). In and through Jesus, however, the very concept of God as law-giver is transformed. Speaking for his Father, Jesus demands of men the kind of behavior that would be a proper response to the Father's love. The God of Christianity is a *demanding* God, precisely because he loves; his demand is the demand of love.

If a Christian's encounter with the risen Christ, through his own prayer and faith and the sharing of that faith with his fellow Christians, is a constant challenge to his understanding of the divine, it is also a challenge to his understanding of "salvation." This would follow naturally from the need to rethink the reality of God; for it is this God, the Father of our Lord Jesus Christ, who is the savior of men. But faith in the risen Christ implies that salvation is not just the work of God; it is also the work of man, and most importantly of this man who has triumphed over evil by his death and resurrection so that men might be saved. Salvation is a divine doing, but it is a divine doing that works through human actions, through what Christ did and does.

This role of Christ in mankind's salvation, a role he now shares with his followers, immediately calls into question that pessimistic view of man which sees him as incapable of contributing positively to his own fulfillment. If one accepts Christian faith, the human activity of Jesus is central to the development of human history; it is indispensable in the process of salvation. At least in Jesus, the human contribution to man's redemption is of undeniable importance. To say that this contribution is dependent upon the divine cooperation is not to say that it is less real or of less value. Moreover, the New Testament books indicate that in lesser degree the same positive judgment can be passed on the actions of other men, for Christ has shared his own saving mission with his disciples: "As my Father has sent me, even so I send you" (Jn. 20:21).

Also, the fact that salvation comes to men through their encounter with Christ, and through him with the Father, indicates that salvation cannot occur without the activity of the one saved. Salvation is received from Christ, but it must be received, it cannot be forced. Because it comes in faith, and faith is a person's free acceptance of the life-giving word of God, salvation requires the free action of the man who is saved. Even God cannot make for a person his own act of faith and love. Salvation is a personal reality, it does not occur magically.

Although such an understanding of "salvation" does not diminish the need for divine intervention to liberate man from evil, it does make clear that this intervention takes place through the human action of Jesus which sacramentalizes the Father's own act. And this understanding does not deny the "supernaturality" of salvation, which is effected through man's response to God's self-gift in Christ; nothing could possibly be more gratuitous and beyond human deserving than this gift of God in personal love. What is stressed in this understanding is the fact that salvation is a mystery of presence: By coming to a man, confronting him in love and gracious forgiveness, giving himself in friendship and fidelity to that man, the risen Christ draws from the man in the response of faith a human integrity and greatness that would not otherwise have been possible.

If "salvation" be understood in this way, as effected in the believer's encounter with the risen Christ, the notion of "sanctity" must be similarly understood. In one way or another, all religions look on "sanctity" as involving some relation to the divinity. In Christianity this relation obviously comes through the experience offered to men in and through the risen Christ. It is not something to be achieved primarily through a person's own efforts to be moral, to avoid contact with evil; it is achieved through God's saving action, to which the person must respond in faith.

One of the constant misunderstandings of sanctity against which the teaching of the New Testament is directed is that sanctity consists in the careful observance of laws. The genuinely holy person will undoubtedly have a profound respect for authentic law, but the New Testament books, particularly Paul's letter to the Romans, insist that observance of law — even the law of the Old Testament — is not sufficient. Instead, it is the law of Christian love, with all its implications, that leads one to true sanctity. The Old Testament exhortation, "be holy, for I the Lord your God am holy" (Lev. 19:2), is translated in Christianity by Jesus' commandment, "love one another as I have loved you" (Jn. 15:12).

Christian sanctity cannot be identified with the notion, drawn from ancient Stoic philosophy, that human perfection can and should be attained by holding oneself aloof from the world, by keeping oneself detached from involvement in the lives and concerns of one's fellowmen and thus remaining "pure" and sinless. There can be no genuine Christian holiness which is not patterned on that of Christ himself. His sanctity is rooted in the reality of the incarnation, and the incarnation is a mystery of God's word becoming thoroughly identified with the human condition — the word came into the world and "became flesh." Jesus himself did not hold aloof from the world of his day. He was so thoroughly involved in ordinary human life that his contemporaries did not suspect his divine identity: "Is not this the carpenter's son?" (Mt. 13:55).

Jesus' mission, the will of his Father, was one of giving himself in redeeming love to men, so that men would live in peace and community. Christianity has no other mission than this. The holiness that is demanded of a Christian, demanded by the encounter with the risen Christ which he shares with his fellow Christians, consists in his participation in the Church's task of making Christ's continuing love present to men. This holiness can involve risks and dangers, for it requires a straightforward confrontation with evil rather than a flight from it. It may even require that one die for the sake of his fellowmen, as Jesus himself had to do.

Only rarely will actual physical death be demanded of a Christian as the expression of his love for others. The constant and unavoidable demand is that of giving himself to others in love and concern. He cannot refuse this and claim to be following the Gospel. "If any one says, 'I love God,' and hates his brother, he is a liar" (1 Jn. 4:20). But if a Christian does live out Christ's commandment of love he has the assurance of living in deepening friendship with Christ and his Father: "If a man loves me, he will keep my word, and my Father will love him, and we will come to him and make our home with him" (Jn. 14:23). For Christians, as for Israel in the Old Testament and for Jesus himself, encounter with God will come about through encounter with human life.

CHAPTER SIX

The People of the New Covenant

CONTEMPORARY MAN'S hopes for a truly human future are largely dependent upon his success or failure in shaping the structures of society. Man, of course, has always found himself in society and has been importantly influenced by it. Yet the rapid increase of population, the accelerating urbanization and mobility of life, the explosive advance of technology and cybernation, have all contributed to an unprecedented fluidity in social structures.

Students of the contemporary scene view the situation with excitement and some alarm. There are unquestionably a number of factors (such as developments in communications) that give great promise for a new unification of mankind. There is also a serious danger of individuals being lost in a vast and depersonalized superstructure. This is not an illusory danger; already in the twentieth century we have seen millions of people caught in a system of collectivism, organized into an anthill existence where they are subordinate to the system, deprived of their fundamental rights and freedom so that some economic or political process could advance. Mankind today may be faced with an unavoidable choice: either establish genuine human *community,* grounded in free cooperation and human sharing, or drift towards a dehumanizing *collectivism.*

Men are searching for ultimate values on which they can build such a genuine human community. The young in particular — though not only they — are distrustful of the value-systems of the West, which have led in our own life-time to genocide and constant war. This would seem to be the logical time for Christians to offer the message of the Gospel as a principle for unifying men, to initiate an effort that would lead to true justice and peace. The disturbing fact is, though, that Christianity is not looked to by most men with any hope; often, just the opposite is true. Many see in "the Protestant ethic" or "the triumphalism" of the Catholic Church partial causes of our social malaise.

Such charges can be answered — perhaps too easily — by saying that Christianity has not failed, it has never been tried. Even if this answer is true, it raises other questions: What is it that should have been tried as an authentic Christian approach to man's social needs? More fundamentally, is there anything about the reality of Christianity, or about the reality of the risen Christ himself, that is meant to affect the manner in which men fashion their society? Is not the influence of Christ, precisely because it operates in the realm of faith, limited to the transformation of individual men?

Community and Individual

Early Christianity, if one can judge its mentality from the New Testament literature, had a definite, though undeveloped, response to these questions. Not only did it believe that the risen Christ was to be the ultimate principle for the unification of mankind, it believed that this formation of human community was to be achieved, somehow, through the corporate life and activity of the Christian community. Thus, a study of Christianity's claim to relevance in the modern world, with its manifold social needs, has two concerns: the role the Christian community can play in the unification of mankind and the way in which Christians themselves are fashioned into community by the risen Christ.

Before going further, it might be well to correct a false opposition that has crept into our posing of the question, and that enters into many discussions of the topic: the opposition between community and individual. It should be obvious that this opposition is not real, at least in the theoretical order. Community demands individuals, and the individual needs a community. In the practicalities of daily life, a tension between individual and group often does develop, with the result that there is a widespread tendency to consider these two as inimical.

Much of the misunderstanding may lie in a faulty identification of "community" with "organized social grouping." Our ordinary use of language seems to reflect this confusion. We speak of the city in which we live as "our community" or we talk about a "community" fund-drive, and in doing so we are referring to the organized political and economic structures in which we fit. Whether or not the human beings who coexist and interact in this particular geographical situation form a genuine human community is quite incidental to our use of the term "community."

Human community exists insofar as a group of people have something in common, insofar as they share something. What they share determines the kind of community they have — a family, a nation, a bowling team. The more personal their sharing, the more profound their community. Among close friends there is a deep experience of community, since what they are sharing most is one another. Among chance acquaintances there is much less community, since there is very little that they truly share with one another.

When genuine and personal community exists, it is clear that it in no way opposes the growth and fulfillment of the individual persons. Just the contrary is the fact, for the individuals grow as persons by their communication with one another. Since a person develops only by relating to other persons, a community in which this interrelationship can occur is of utmost importance for a person. Without such a community, one cannot establish one's own identity.

We already saw some of this as applicable to Christianity when we examined (in the last chapter) the manner in which the faith of the believing community acts as a criterion for the faith-judgment of the individual Christian. At that point our interest was in showing the manner in which this community of faith can serve to establish the reality of the risen Christ, so that the individual believer can believe and so discover his identity as a Christian in relation to Christ. But one also identifies himself as a Christian in relation to his fellow believers. He is one of those who share faith in Christ and who express that faith in their life and worship.

A community of faith is necessary if the individual is to have faith. If this were the only, or even the principal, purpose for the existence of the Church, however, it would mean that Christianity was an introverted and self-centered form of religion; one could not expect any help from it in solving the problems of mankind's social existence. Occasionally, such a narcissistic view of the Church's life does gain some prominence among groups of Christians, and needs to be offset by reflection on the view found in the New Testament writings. In our own day, the Second Vatican Council resoundingly rejected this self-centered interpretation of Christianity, especially in its Pastoral Constitution on the Church in the Modern World.

In insisting on the apostolic orientation of the Church, and on the fact that the Church is essentially a community of believers, "the people of God," Vatican II, particularly in the Constitution on the Church, was quite clearly dependent upon the mentality of the New Testament writers. Drawing from the outlook contained in Scripture, the bishops of Vatican II emphasized the corporate and social aspects of human salvation.

The New Adam

One of the New Testament themes that points to the social nature of salvation is that of Christ as "the new Adam" (Rom. 5). Though not found exclusively in the Pauline literature, this parallel between Jesus and Adam is prominent in Paul's thought and is linked with his understanding of Christ as "the first-born" or as "the head of creation."

Though he attempts no philosophical or theological analysis of the fact, Paul sees some kind of community existing throughout the entire human race. Not only do all men share the same way of existence, they also share the same sad fate of death and all that is associated with death. At the root of this common subjection to death lies the communion of men in sin. From the beginning of mankind's existence on this earth, men have sinned; the first man began it, and men since then have joined their own sinfulness to his. There is, then, a common burden of sin that all men bear, and to which all men contribute, and this means that there is a shared need for redemption.

It is in answer to this universal need that Jesus comes as redeemer. Just as sin and death entered human history through Adam's sin, so through Christ's death and resurrection the gracious mercy of God comes to save men and to give them life. Salvation in Christ does not come to men automatically; they must ally themselves to him in faith, just as they ally themselves with the first Adam by their own sin. But the reality of the risen Christ, who has triumphed over death and sin, makes it possible for men to link themselves with him and so share in the life-giving mercy of his Father.

Paul's comparison of the risen Christ with Adam shows that redemption reaches out beyond the Christian community to touch all men. As extensive as mankind's community in death is its community in the everlasting life that Christ has won by his death. Salvation is open to each man, but in some fashion (which the early Church did not clarify) this must come through union with Christ in faith. There is only one savior, only one mediator to the Father, Christ Jesus (1 Tim. 2:5). Men reach their destiny only by sharing with Christ that inheritance of unending life with the Father to which he laid claim in his death and resurrection.

One would miss the deeper level of Paul's thought on Jesus as the "second Adam" if he understood this to mean only that Jesus' obedience unto death merited salvation for all men. The mystery of Christ's role is imbedded in the very structures of human existence. The life he now has as the risen Lord is shared — one might almost say "physically shared" — with men. Just as ancient peoples saw the oldest son of a family as somehow possessing the whole life-force of the family, so the risen Christ who is the "first-born from the dead" possesses that new life that flows out to enliven his fellow men (1 Cor. 15:20-23).

The deepest unity of mankind, then, is grounded in Christ. It was to effect this unity that he suffered, died, and rose to new life (Eph. 2:13-16). It is to carry out effectively this communication of life that he still works through the community of faith which is the Church. Christians exist as a community, sharing Christ's life and his life-giving Spirit, so that they can help fashion all men into a community of life.

The New Israel

If the early Christians saw themselves in relationship to the entire human race, they also saw themselves as specially related to Old Testament Israel. The exact nature of this relationship was something that they never fully worked out, though it was grounded in the fact that the Yahweh who guided Old Testament history was the same god whom the Christians recognized as the Father of Christ. In general, the early decades of Christian faith looked on both Jesus and the early Church as the fulfillment of Israel.

There is no doubt that the primitive Christian communities not only did not fit within the structured organization of Jewish religion, but increasingly dissociated themselves from official Judaism. Reaction against the Judaizing tendencies of some within the Christian group strengthened this split with Judaism. Despite this fact, the New Testament literature gives clear evidence that the early Christians looked upon themselves as "the new Israel."

Since this continuity with Old Testament Israel was not one of structures or organization, it is evident that the link was on a deeper level, that of Israel's identity as "the people of God." Within Old Testament history there is an opposition between two ways of identifying Israel: as a people or as a nation. Israel finds her identity on the basis of her political structure and economic alliances, and so looks upon herself as a nation among other nations; or (as the great prophets urge) she finds her identity as a group of people united because of their election by Yahweh. It is with Israel identified in this second fashion that early Christianity feels itself in continuity; it, too, is essentially a people, called into being by the death and resurrection of Jesus, which is the new passover.

Much of the early Church's understanding of herself as "new Israel" was linked with her belief that Jesus was the long-awaited Messiah of the Old Testament Israelites. The earliest forms of the kerygma proclaimed Jesus in his resurrection as being the Messiah (Acts 2:36), and the Gospels reflect the manner in which Christian thought realized that Jesus fulfilled the messianic expectations in enigmatic fashion: by being a suffering servant, the fulfillment of the prophetic movement, and the Son of Man. Contrary as was his messiahship to the expectations of the Jews, it was related by early Christian faith to the traditions of the Old Testament scriptures. The phrase "so that the scriptures might be fulfilled" is a recurrent theme in the Gospel descriptions of the deeds of Jesus.

If Jesus was the Messiah, the early Christians formed the messianic community, the final stage of Israel's development. In a true sense they were already the eschatological community, the kingdom of the saints that had been foretold in the book of Daniel, just as Jesus himself was the Son of Man, the very personification of that kingdom of the saints

(Dan. 7). Small wonder, then, that some in those early decades of Christianity anticipated the imminent end of the world and the "second coming" of Christ.

Another Old Testament notion that the early Christians utilized to explain their relationship to Judaism was that of "the remnant." They may well have done so in their attempt to puzzle through what for them was a painful mystery: the fact that a relatively small portion of the Jews accepted Jesus as the Christ, the Messiah. Looking backward to their Old Testament traditions, they would have found the notion of "the remnant" in Isaiah and on through the prophetic writings. This was the idea that much of Israel would prove unfaithful to Yahweh, and that on the "day of the Lord" only a small remnant of the faithful would remain to be the nucleus of the restored people. Now, when the final "day of the Lord" had dawned with the resurrection of Jesus, the prophecies were being fulfilled. Again, only a few prove themselves open to the word that God speaks to them. As so often in the past, Israel does not know her Lord; the Word came to his own people and they did not accept him (Jn. 1:11). But from those who do accept him as Messiah there will arise a renewed and fulfilled Israel, a new people of God that has inherited the promises made to Abraham.

Probably the clearest and most detailed indication of the early Church's identification of herself as "new Israel" is her belief that Jesus had established the new covenant in his death and resurrection. As it is described in the Gospel traditions, the Last Supper is really the first (and indispensable) stage in this new passover event which then proceeds to Calvary and resurrection. It is at the Supper that Jesus takes the cup and says, repeating Moses' words at Sinai, "this is the blood of the covenant." Only in this case it is the "blood of the *new* covenant."

Israel's traditions over the centuries regarded the enactment of the covenant as the root of her existence as a people. The enactment of a new covenant would suggest the bringing into being of a new people of God. This would not necessarily be by way of denying the older Mosaic dispensation; rather, the new would mark the fulfillment of what preceded it — "not one jot or tittle of the Law will pass away until it all be fulfilled." Yet it would mean that the Christian covenant had superseded the Israelitic one, and men would no longer worship in the Temple according to the Mosaic covenant law. Instead they would gather to celebrate the eucharistic reenactment of the new covenant (Jn. 4:21-24).

Their frequent gathering to celebrate the eucharistic "breaking of the bread" bears witness to the centrality of the idea of "covenant people" in the faith of the early Christians. It would have been practically impossible for them to share the cup of "the blood of the new covenant" and not be aware of themselves as the new Israel formed by that covenant. In this action they would have discovered their identity as a community of faith, the people of God.

Primitive Christianity clearly felt the need to establish its continuity with the salvation history of Old Testament Israel. Essentially this continuity was provided by Jesus himself, who was the realization of all Israel's ideals. But the early Christians increasingly felt the need to distinguish themselves from Judaism, a process that was probably intensified by the destruction of the Temple and Jerusalem in 70 A.D. That raised the question, a question that remains to some extent for each generation of Christians to answer: What is it most basically that constitutes Christianity as a unique kind of community? If it claims to be distinctive, as it does, what is the principle of its distinctiveness?

Faith-consciousness

In a sense, the response of the New Testament literature is disarmingly simple: The distinctive principle of Christianity as a community is the risen Christ himself. The situation, as they see it, is both similar to and different from that which had existed for Israel during the Old Testament period. In the last analysis, the characteristic identity of Israel was established in relationship to the god, Yahweh, whom the Israelites worshipped and whose presence to them transformed their world view and their understanding of themselves. So, too, the distinctive identity of the primitive Christian community was discovered in relationship to this same god of the Old Testament, whom they now saw revealed as the Father of the Lord Jesus, and to the risen Christ himself, who shared divinity with his Father. But there was a profound difference, too. The Christians believed that Christ was formative of their community in a much more intimate and intrinsic manner; he was actually one of the community himself, and unified its members "from within" the group.

This early Christian viewpoint bears careful examination, for if it is what it seems, it reveals as useless such a question as: Why have the Church? Why not simply have a situation in which believers can contact Christ directly? Apparently, in the mentality we find reflected in the New Testament books, the situation in which a believer can contact Christ is, precisely, in the Christian community. To test the validity of this interpretation of early Christian faith, it will be necessary to look at several aspects of New Testament teaching: the unity of Christians in faith and in the Spirit of Christ, the Church's continuation of Jesus' role as priest and prophet, the Christian community as body and sacrament of Christ.

To read the New Testament writings is to become inescapably aware that a common consciousness, which they refer to by the term "faith," bound the early Christians into community. There were differences of opinion as to the exact meaning of Christ, at times even bitter differences as to what was required for Christian life; but always there was a deeply shared awareness of the reality of the risen Lord, an awareness of his presence to them, an awareness of the working of his Spirit in their midst.

As we mentioned in an earlier chapter, this faith had come into being with the transforming experience of Easter.

This event so affected the consciousness of those who shared in it, that their entire view of reality became changed — and continued to change as they reflected on the implications of the event. Besides, they immediately went out to tell others "the good news," and so share with them this awareness in faith of the risen Christ. Christian communities came into being through this preaching of the Gospel.

It was not as though a message of marvelous promise — which, of course, the Gospel was — held them together, a message about what Jesus had said and done. Rather, it was Christ himself whose presence and love they shared with one another. It was their community in his presence that they expressed and celebrated when they gathered "in his name" for the breaking of the bread.

But the experience of shared consciousness of the risen Christ reached into the depths of mystery, the very mystery of divine life and divine consciousness. For the New Testament writings, particularly the Acts of the Apostles, tell us that the early Christians were aware of sharing Christ's own Spirit. They were bound into personal community because one Spirit permeated their consciousness as individuals and as a group.

We do have instances, some of them productive, some of them disastrous, in our human history of men, possessed of charismatic powers of leadership, who were able to communicate their own attitudes and hopes and ambitions, their own "spirit," to other men and thus bind them powerfully together. This kind of occurrence, though on a new level, marked the life of the early Christians. With his passage into risen life Jesus, even as man, shared fully in the Spirit of his Father; and the Spirit he now shares with his followers.

In utterly unique fashion, then, the early Christians were linked to one another in community by their sharing of one Spirit, the Spirit of Christ and of his Father, which became truly their own Spirit. This is the essence of the event of Pentecost: the Holy Spirit becomes the animating principle of the community of believers that is the Church. From this source the Christian community draws its life of faith in Christ, its filial relationship to the Father, its power to transform human history by love, its own social unity.

This unity effected by Christ's Spirit was a conscious, experienced unity. It was a unity of mind and heart with the risen Christ himself and therefore with one another. John's Gospel points out that it is the function of this Spirit to form the minds of Christians to that of Christ himself (Jn. 14:26); Paul exhorts the Philipians, "Have this mind among yourselves, which was in Christ Jesus . . ." (Phil. 2:5). The presence of the Spirit whom the risen Christ gives to the Church is in no way a replacement of Christ's own presence. There is one mystery of presence by which the risen Lord makes himself present to his followers in the gift of his Spirit.

The New Testament literature makes it quite clear that the union of Christians with the risen Christ is direct and immediate, something more than might have been produced in a group of men and women who had been inspired by what Jesus had done and shared his spirit in that sense. Some kind of immediate communication of life from Christ to his followers is certainly indicated by the fifteenth chapter of John's Gospel: Jesus speaks of himself as the true vine whose very life force flows into the branches, his disciples. This is no doubt a figurative way of speaking, and we should also remember that the sixth chapter of that same Gospel speaks of Jesus bringing life to those who will believe in him as "the word." There is still a view reflected in John 15 which considers the union between Christ and his followers as almost physical in nature, certainly as involving continued presence to one another: "Abide in me, and I in you."

This same mentality pervades the Pauline letters. The Christian community is built upon the cornerstone who is Christ (Eph. 2:20-22). The Christian community is the bride espoused by Christ, who has given himself to her in his death and resurrection so that he might bring her to the full beauty he desires for her (Eph. 5:25-27). So close is the union and identity between Christ and his Church that they form one body, he the head and they the members (Eph. 4:15-16). It would be almost impossible to explain the use of such language if there was not in the early Church a belief in the constant presence of the risen Lord to Christians.

The unity of Christians and Christ is a dynamic one. Those who accept the risen Christ in faith and are thus united with him share in his redeeming ministry. Those who believe the kerygma, the message of Christ's death and resurrection, are themselves caught up into that event. They co-suffer with Christ, co-die with him, and are co-risen with him. Baptism is an action of dying, being buried, and rising with Christ. Use of such "co-" words (from the Greek prefix *syn-)* is a characteristic of Paul's writings, but it is essentially the same idea that is contained in John 15, where Jesus exhorts his disciples to remain united to him so that they may bear much fruit.

Christians, then, form a profound and intimate community with the risen Lord, and therefore with one another. They share Christ's own life; they participate in his own redeeming activity; and with him they share the inheritance proper to his own sonship, the destiny of unending union with his Father. Many other factors helped to forge the early Christians into a closely knit human group, not least the persecution they began quite early to experience. But that which lay at the very root of their shared life and consciousness was the reality of the risen Christ himself.

United in this faith in the risen Christ, united also in life and activity and destiny, the early Christians were inescapably set apart from their contemporaries. Looking back on the early Christians from our twentieth-century vantage point we can describe the process by which they were differentiated from others as a process of Christianization; they were changed by the reality of Christ himself. For the early Christians themselves, immediately immersed in the experiences of those early Christian decades, it was less easy to establish with clarity the elements that constituted their distinctive social self-identity.

A People Set Apart

Paul's epistles provide evidence that the Christians soon became conscious of being a select group; they are "the saints." To modern ears the use of this term can smack of arrogance, of a claim to moral and religious superiority. However, this does not seem to be the context in which the early followers of the risen Christ used the expression. For them, the term indicated their belief that they had, independently of their merits, been singled out for the gift of faith in the risen Christ. More than once, Paul points out to his auditors that the call to faith had come to them when they were "still in their sins." If they were numbered among "the saints," this could be attributed only to the mercy of the Father who had called them in Christ Jesus.

Their union with one another and with Christ, gratuitous as it was, did effect a drastic change in them. The vision of human life that they shared, the ideal of human behavior to which they were now called, the values to which they were committed, were of a new and more exalted order. They shared in the transformation of human life and experience that was achieved in the resurrection of Christ, for it was into this resurrection that they were initiated through their baptism.

More radically, they were set apart by their possession of the Spirit of Christ, the sanctifying Spirit. Yahweh, who had made himself in a special manner present to the Jerusalem Temple, and so had consecrated it, had made himself much more present in the man Jesus. To him, his own son incarnated, he had imparted the fullness of his Spirit, thus sanctifying Jesus in a unique fashion and making him the source of sanctification for all mankind. With the resurrection of Jesus, culminating in Pentecost, it is the Christian community that becomes "the Temple of the Spirit," specially consecrated by the indwelling presence of Christ and his Spirit (1 Cor. 3:16).

Whether one accepts the reality of what the early Christians believed or not, namely that they were a community set apart from others by the presence of Christ and his Spirit, the historical fact is that they did possess this idea and that it was a central factor in their social self-awareness. While entry into the Christian community and adherence in faith to the mystery of Christ's death and resurrection was dependent upon each person's decision, it was God who had drawn them together and elected them as his own people, "the new Israel."

As such a consecrated community, the Christians could act as a principle of sacralization in the world, in a manner both similar to and different from that in which Old Testament Israel functioned. For the people of the Old Testament, the experience of space and time had been altered by their faith in the presence and action of Yahweh. "The world" as a context of their life and consciousness was made sacred by their awareness of Yahweh. The land in which they lived, especially the "holy city" of Jerusalem and its Temple, was a sacred place because Yahweh worked there to bless his people. The events of Israel's history formed a "salvation history" that put all time in a different perspective.

With the resurrection of Jesus and his presence to the Christian community, this Old Testament process is deepened and fulfilled. The mystery of divine presence to men is revealed now as the intimate relationship of the Father to men in and through his Son and Spirit. This presence is no longer tied to any special sacred place; wherever there are Christians who accept in faith the abiding reality of the risen Christ and his Father, there is a special presence of

God (Jn. 14:23). The Church itself, not some building, is the new temple in which the glory of the Father is manifest.

For the Christian, then, the spatial world in which he experiences life is permeated by the presence of the risen Christ, his Father, and their Spirit. This is much more than a realization that the creative power of the Almighty sustains and directs all the forces of the universe; it is the awareness that Christ and his Father abide with Christians (and through them with all men) in loving familiarity. Because they are one body with the risen Lord, because they are animated by his own Spirit — and therefore are a uniquely consecrated reality — Christians themselves are a source of sacralization for the world of which they are a part.

The sequence of events that makes up the Church's pilgrimage through time stands somehow at the center of mankind's history. It is a sacred thread that runs through the complex evolution of man's existence in time, giving it meaning and ultimate purpose in relation to the risen Christ. The history of the Church and the evolution of its life of faith and hope and love, involved with and involving the broader development of mankind as a whole, is meant to be a process of working out in human life the implications of the death and resurrection of Christ. This does not mean that the risen Christ gives over to the Christian community the task of continuing *after him* the work he began; he remains active in human history, working in and through the Christian community to which he is dynamically present.

Perhaps one might distinguish the New Testament from the Old Testament state of sacralization by saying that the former is more "intrinsic." During the centuries of Israel's career, God watched over this people, guided and directed and protected them, but always, as it were, from "outside." Yahweh himself was never a part of the people. In the New Testament situation, on the contrary, the risen Christ works intrinsically. He himself is immanent to the life of the community; he functions as the "head of the body" and communicates to it his own animating Spirit. The providential guidance of history in the Christian era is from the "inside."

Mankind's experience of space and time is meant, then, to be changed by the presence of the risen Christ to the Church. It must be remembered, however, that this is something that occurs only through faith, through the Christian community's conscious acceptance of the reality of the risen Lord, present and active in its life. Presence in the true sense can exist only when there is conscious communication of some kind between persons. Christ's presence to his followers is dependent upon their awareness in faith of his self-gift to them. If they are aware of Christ's gift of self, and accept him in friendship, their experience of life becomes changed and enriched. The world in which they live and the time in which they move become filled with his presence, the experience of human life becomes Christianized.

One thing is plain from a reading of the New Testament literature. If the Christian community is set apart by the presence of Christ and his Spirit, if it is specially chosen and consecrated, this is so that this community can turn outside itself and bring to other men the power of Christ's presence. At times, the Church can forget this "outer-directedness" which is basic to its existence; it can focus too much on its own intrinsic growth and organization. It needs, then, to be reminded of its function in history, which is to be for the sake of others. The Second Vatican Council was such a reminder, particularly in its documents on the Church and on the Church's role in the modern world.

A Prophetic and Priestly Community

Vatican II, in speaking of the role of the Church in human life today, follows the traditional view of the Christian community as a *prophetic* and *priestly one*. Obviously, to describe the Church's functions in terms of these two types of activity is to follow the Scriptures. In the Old

Testament books we already find the belief that the entire people of Israel, not just certain selected individuals, is in some sense priestly and prophetic. Primitive Christianity sees the prophetic and priestly role of Christ extended to that community of believers through which he continues to act.

When one talks about the mentality of the early Church regarding the Christian role of "priesthood," one must be careful not to read into that mentality the Old Testament notions of priesthood, or for that matter the notions of priesthood that have developed during the past few centuries. Apart from the epistle to the Hebrews, the New Testament literature does not use the word "priest" of Christ, and even Hebrews is intent on contrasting the priesthood of Christ with that of the Old Testament Temple. One cannot draw from this the conclusion that early Christianity did not think of Christ, or of itself, as continuing Christ's deeds in terms of priesthood. But the idea of priestly activity is less narrowly cultic than it was in Old Testament thought; it extends more broadly to the whole of human life.

The idea of "priesthood" in a broad sense seems to be inescapably bound up with the notion of "worship," and worship is, in one form or another, the acknowledgment of a divinity. For Old Testament Israel, this was a question of acknowledging Yahweh, the god who had brought the Israelites out of Egypt, as the only god. In Christianity it is a matter of acknowledging the Father of Christ, Christ himself, and the Spirit.

For the early Christians, whose outlook is reflected in the New Testament literature, Jesus himself was the model for acknowledgement of the Father and therefore the beginning of a new approach to "priesthood." Though he undoubtedly participated in the great religious festivals and in the regular Temple worship of his day, he is never depicted by the New Testament writers in these cultic situations. They point instead, to the fact that his worship, that is his acknowledgment of his Father as a divine person, is much more basic and all-embracing.

Jesus' acknowledgment of his Father consisted in the acceptance, total and joyful, of the concrete life-situation that was his. This basic attitude towards the realities of his human life was the best possible expression of his attitude towards his Father; it made clear that he trusted his Father's love for him, his Father's wisdom, and his Father's power. Though he did give cultic expression to this attitude at times — specifically at the Last Supper — the worship of his Father included his entire attitude towards reality: one of grateful acceptance. Such an attitude is not a passive one; it is, as the Gospels make clear in their description of Jesus, a mature acceptance of the responsibilities dictated by a person's life-circumstances.

So, too, is the priestly worship of the Christian community. Though it finds special expression in an action such as the Eucharist, it is meant to extend to the whole of life. As Paul writes to the Corinthian Christians (1 Cor. 10:31): "So whether you eat or drink, or whatever you do, do all to the glory of God." Like Christ himself, Christians are meant to trust the loving care and wisdom of their heavenly Father, thus giving witness to their faith that he is truly "Father." In this fashion the entire Christian people is meant to exercise the priestly task of acknowledging the true God.

This may well seem, at first sight, to be a task divorced from ordinary human life and the practical demands of daily human existence. Just the contrary: It consists in an optimistic and hopeful seizing of the responsibilities dictated by a given historical situation. It is an attitude meant to permeate the individual and community activity of Christians, an attitude that finds appropriate expression in the action of the Eucharist because "Eucharist" means "a giving of thanks."

Inseparably linked with their priestly role is the Christians' function of prophecy, for prophecy, too, is a matter of bearing witness to the Father of Christ. Indeed, it would be artificial to attempt a sharp distinction between the two functions. Christ himself, who not only is the model of Christian priesthood and prophecy but also continues to exercise these roles through his presence to the Christian community, had united in his earthly ministry the Old Testament ideals of prophet and priest and king and in so doing had given them a new and transformed meaning.

The New Testament writers, intent on explaining the meaning of Christian faith and life, did single out the prophetic activity of Jesus as a key aspect of his earthly ministry. Not just in his public teaching, where he is clearly compared with the Old Testament prophets, is Jesus described as "the great prophet." More importantly, in his identification of himself as "the Servant" (as described in the Isaian "Servant Songs") and in his fulfillment of that servant role by his death and resurrection, Jesus becomes the realization of Old Testament prophecy, since the figure of "the Servant" is the idealization of the prophetic role in Israel.

As the faith of the early Church views him, Jesus is not just the most perfect prophet; he is Word made flesh. Yahweh's word had been on the lips of the Old Testament prophets. In Jesus, the Father speaks his own Word, a totally adequate one, and he speaks him humanly, in the mystery of enfleshment (Jn. 1:1-14). Not only the words and deeds of Jesus speak for and witness to his Father, which they do, but everything he is as a man is a translation into human form of his divine identity as the Son and the Word of the Father. The entire human life and experience and activity of Jesus was therefore prophetic in this deeper sense; as no other human possibly could, he "spoke for God."

It was in the context of this mystery of the Word-made-flesh that the early Christians understood their own prophetic role. They were to proclaim the "good news," the Gospel, of Jesus' death and resurrection, that is Jesus' own supreme human word to men. More than that, they were to live out in their own lives and deaths the mystery of Christ's death and resurrection, and thus give witness to the continuing redemptive efficacy of Christ's passover (Rom. 6:1-14). Their total human experience and activity was to bear witness to Christ and his Father, to speak for them to the world, to be prophetic.

The prophetic role of the Christian community goes still deeper; it shares in the mystery of the incarnation of the Father's own Word. By her preaching and her life the Church speaks to the world about the mystery of Christ, but she is meant to go beyond that and to make present to men the Word who is Christ, so that he can himself continue to bear witness to his Father. As the early Christians understood it, the Church is able to do this because she is the bride and the body of the risen Christ.

It is Paul in particular (though not exclusively) who utilizes the Old Testament prophetic theme of Yahweh as the husband of Israel, and applies it to the relationship between Christ and the Christian community as a means of understanding the profundity and intimacy of that relationship (Eph. 5:20-25). The Christian community is the bride to whom Jesus has committed himself in a total self-gift through his death and resurrection. He willingly chose to give up the human life he had known in his earthly career, so that he might share a new life — and, in a sense, a new identity — with his followers. Just as a husband and wife, in their loving gift of self to one another, become (in the words of Genesis) "one flesh," the risen Christ and his Church become one body. The Christian people is the Body of Christ, not in some vague coalescence through which distinctiveness and identity are lost, but in the paradox of personal love in which both the identification and the distinctiveness of the partners is meant to grow in intensity.

Because the Church is the body of Christ, it is the embodiment of the Word (Eph. 4). The Church is not itself the Word incarnate, but through its profound identification in love with Christ, who is that incarnated Word, the Church does become an extension of the mystery of incarnation. Thus, it can in its prophetic function actually bring mankind into contact with the Word himself. Analogous to the manner in which our own human bodiliness is the instrumentality through which we communicate with other persons — a way that makes it possible to share our consciousness with others and give ourselves to others in friendship — the risen Christ is able to give himself to men in life-giving communication through his body which is the Christian community.

The prophetic activity of the Church is, then, the prophetic activity of the risen Christ himself. In and through Christians, both in their individual lives and in their existence together as a community of faith, the risen incarnated Word continues to speak to the world the saving love of his Father. To put it another way, the Father continues to speak his Word to men through the Church. This saving action of the Father in sending his life-giving Word takes place in proportion to the unity of consciousness between Christ and his followers, in proportion to the Church's depth and accuracy of faith. Paul's exhortation to the Philippian community has great practical importance: "Have this mind . . . which was in Christ Jesus. . . ."

There is another aspect of the Church's witness to Christ and to his Father which one can see if he joins two ideas from Paul's letters, two ideas that Paul apparently does not himself formally connect. The first is that which we have already studied, namely that the Church is the Bride of Christ. The other is expressed in the first epistle to the Corinthians, where Paul says that "man is the image and glory of God, but woman is the glory of man."

What can it mean to say that "woman is the glory of man"? Without trying to limit ourselves exclusively to the strict exegetical question — what, exactly, did Paul intend to say by this clause? — there does seem to be an avenue of profitable reflection on this text that remains within the thought-world of Paul and the early Christians. In the Bible the term "the glory of God" has a long history and a quite precise meaning. What it refers to is "the redeeming intent and power of God *as manifested*." Thus a man, insofar as he manifested the saving power of God in his life, could be called the glory of God, even though, in this case, the phrase was not applied to men.

If we transfer this meaning to the man-woman relationship of which Paul speaks, a wife could be said to be the glory of her husband if in her person and life she manifested the saving influence he had had on her. The peace of mind, the maturity, the psychological security, the capacity to love, the joy that she possessed would all point to the beneficial effectiveness of her husband's love. Her very being would bear witness to the greatness of her husband as a person.

The same is true of the Christian community with respect to Christ, whose bride she is. The men and women who make up the Christian Church should be transformed, fulfilled, redeemed by the liberating power of Christ's love for them. There should be in the Christian community an abiding peace and happiness and hope that tells men about the influence of the risen Christ and attracts them to him. By its whole life the Christian community should preach the Gospel; in so doing, it is truly the glory of the risen Lord.

A Sacramental Community

As we mentioned earlier, the Constitution on the Church from Vatican II emphasizes biblical imagery and thought in its explanation of the Church, so that we would expect to find it speaking, as it does, of the priestly and prophetic character of the Christian people. It adds another idea which is not contained as such in the New Testament writings, but which grows out of New Testament thought: the Church is "the sacrament" of Christ. Most Christians in recent centuries have grown accustomed to the use of "sacrament" for ritual actions, such as Baptism or the Eucharist, so that the application of the term to the Church may seem strange.

Few words, if any, could more appropriately be used to describe the nature and activity of the Christian Church. A sacrament is a sign; it conveys a meaning, a significance. It is different from other signs in that it effects the very reality it signifies. Baptism, for example, not only points to the new Christian's union with the risen Christ, it achieves that union. So with the Church: It not only indicates by its existence and activity that the risen Christ is still present to men in history, it makes him present through its life of faith. Because Christians through their acceptance in faith admit the influence of Christ to their consciousness, he is able to be personally present to them and through them to the world.

We must not forget that presence is not primarily a matter of being located in space, of "being there." Most deeply, it is a matter of persons giving themselves personally to one another through some form of communication; it is a matter of "being *for*." Christ's risen presence to men is a mystery of his being *for* them; it is his gift of himself to them so that they may live. The Christian community must signify this gift through its own life, if it is truly to function as sacrament, and it does so through its own corporate love for men.

God the Father (as John 3:16 tells us) so loved the world, that he sent his own Son, his own Word, to bring eternal life to men. That Son did speak of his Father's love and witnessed to it by his death and resurrection. The Christian community is also meant to be a sign, a "word," that speaks prophetically to men the message of the Father's love. This it will do by loving as Christ did: "This is my commandment, that you love one another as I have loved you." In fulfilling this commandment, the Christian people become "the light of the world."

Again, the very existence of the Church as a true human community of believers in Christ signifies the kind of activity that the risen Lord carries on in history. This activity of the risen Christ, which is the heart of his priestly function, is one of bringing all men into a community. He is the Prince of Peace, who works to achieve among all men a situation of justice, mutual trust, and basic equality. He desires all men to be one family under the fatherhood of his own Father.

All this the Church is meant as sacrament to signify and help effect. To a world of men that is skeptical at best about the possibilities of human beings ever living in peace and harmony, the Church is meant to stand as a sign that genuine and free human community is possible. What the Christian community indicates, however, is that such unification comes through the redeeming action of Christ. If Christians form a community, it is because of their acceptance in faith of the risen Christ. If Christians share a common spirit — and every truly human community must have some common spirit — it is because the risen Lord is sharing his own Spirit with them.

For the Christian community to manifest the community-forming work of the risen Christ, it itself must clearly be seen as a truly unified group of men and women. This, of course, is the tragic deficiency of our present situation: The Church, which should be the great sacrament of human unification, is itself splintered into differing (even opposing) denominations. Gratifyingly, some of the bitter enmity between these groups which has led to venomous polemics, social bigotry, and even war (all in the name of Christ!) is dissipating, and there is hope that Christians may once more be united with one another.

Because the Christian people is meant by its own unity to be the sign that effects unity among all men, the ecumenical efforts of the present moment are of critical importance. Until the Church can manifest by its own life the unifying power of the Spirit of Christ, it cannot effectively fulfill its own prophetic role of announcing the transforming presence of the risen Christ, nor can it function fully as the instrument of Christ's priestly work of uniting mankind.

To say that the Church is not adequately functioning as the sacrament of Christ's unifying activity is not to say that it fails utterly in this regard. History is a process of human beings slowly inching toward the kind of freedom and maturity that should mark them as persons. The Christian community is composed of men living in this historical process. The Church is moving towards that ideal situation when it will completely sacramentalize the unifying activity of the risen Christ. When it reaches that ideal, we will have come to the Parousia.

We might reflect also on the fact that the Christian community will more healthily achieve its own unification if it does not turn its attention inward, directing all its attention to its own internal development, but rather looks outward to the task of unifying mankind. People are unified by working together toward a common goal; to the degree the Church is involved in the task of bringing genuine unity in peace and justice to mankind, the Church will become a true Christian community. Ultimately, only the risen Christ is the unifying principle who can form all men into one human family; only he, who is the unique Son of God the Father, can share his own sonship with men and thereby unite them under one Father. But Christ does this through the Church, which by its efforts to bring unity to men sacramentalizes — makes effectively present — Christ's own action of unifying men.

A Community of Persons

The Christian people is meant, then, to be unified by its corporate exercise of the priestly and prophetic functions that are proper to it as the body of Christ. Its capacity to perform these functions in the profound sacramental way we have been discussing requires something beyond mere functional unification; it requires a truly personal community among the men and women who make up the Church. In order to act in unified and unifying fashion, Christians themselves must be one in heart and mind. That does not mean that there must exist some monolithic identity of thought and viewpoint; what must exist is the kind of mature love for one another which permits a genuine pluralism in understanding to enrich rather than endanger the group's unity.

Early Christianity seems to have been very aware of the need for this truly personal level of community. The New Testament literature is filled with exhortations, explicit and implicit, to mutual love and concern. One thinks immediately of the Johannine writings: of the first letter of John, almost totally devoted to the theme of fraternal love — "This is the message that you have heard from the beginning, that we should love one another"; or of the last discourse of Jesus in John's Gospel, with its repeated emphasis on the loving unity that Jesus wishes for his disciples — "A new commandment I give to you, that you love one another" (Jn. 13:34).

But this is not a peculiarly Johannine theme. Paul's letters are filled with expressions of his own loving concern for his many close friends in the various Christian communities, and with expressions of his anguished desire that Christians live with one another in open and honest love. When that kind of unity was threatened by selfish interests or partisan disputes or class distinctions, Paul could write (as he did to the Corinthians) in sharp, even caustic, language. He realized that only the bond of love could resolve the tensions that are built into the Church's life and structure. No more beautiful eulogy of love has been written than the thirteenth chapter of 1 Corinthians, yet Paul's purpose in writing it was eminently practical.

Some, perhaps many, people in the Church today are disturbed by what they think is an undue emphasis on "the commandment of love" in contemporary theological writing. This reaction is no doubt due partially to an excessively legalistic religious formation. It may also be reaction to sentimentalism about "Christian community" that one does occasionally encounter—a superficial understanding of Christian love that can lay no claim either to scriptural foundation or to theological justification. But to see an emphasis on genuine human love as a threat to Christian faith is to ignore utterly the New Testament scriptures.

It would be naive and unhistorical to picture the life of the early Christian communities as one of unbroken harmony and tranquility; the very frequency of the exhortations in those communities to work towards these blessings suggests that they were not always present! On the other hand, when one reads through the New Testament literature he can sense the close bond of mutual concern and love that linked the early Christians with one another. As he is described in the Gospels, Jesus himself felt and manifested a deep human affection for the people with whom he dealt, particularly for his disciples; this created among them a spirit of brotherhood, which he was intensely interested in fostering. What he had begun during the relatively brief period of his public ministry, he completed by sending his own Spirit in the mystery of Pentecost.

Christianity is meant, then, to be essentially a community of persons united with the risen Christ and sharing his Spirit, and therefore united with one another. Already in the Old Testament period of revelation the prophets of Israel had insisted that true acceptance of the covenant with Yahweh involved equality and justice among the people. This was exactly what Yahweh was doing: He was forming a people for himself. So strong was the emphasis on this relationship among the Israelites themselves, that from Amos onward the prophets constantly link social injustice with idolatry as the great sins of the people; at times the prophets almost identify these two sins.

One finds the same emphasis in the New Testament writings, only now in terms of preserving and developing the unity that should characterize the body of Christ. Paul's moral catechesis concentrates to a great extent upon the relationships of Christians one to another. Those who make up the body of Christ should live together in open honesty, in respect for one another's dignity and rights, without strife or enmity or jealous contention; they should be watchful for one another's needs, whether material or spiritual; they should work to preserve the bond of charity that gives expression to the presence of Christ's own spirit of love (Rom. 12:1-15:13).

The Gospels trace such exhortations back to the teaching of Jesus himself. Those who accept him in faith and thereby accept the word that the Father is speaking to them, really form one family under that Father and in union with Christ. "Whoever does the will of my Father in heaven is my brother and sister and mother" (Mt. 12:50). One can, of course, pass over such statements lightly, seeing in them only the exaggeration of rhetorical emphasis. Careful study of the New Testament writings, however, indicates that they are to be taken as profoundly true; Christians are assumed there to be so intimately linked with the risen Christ in a sharing of life that they are his brothers and his sisters and therefore such to one another.

Just as Israel's prophets pointed out the emptiness and hypocrisy of worship performed by men who violated the rights and persons of their fellow men, the New Testament writings describe the vanity of worship that is not accompanied by fraternal charity. If a man comes to offer his gift to God in worship and remembers that his brother has some grievance against him, there is no point in continuing with his act or worship; it is meaningless. Unless he is willing to acknowledge his brother as brother, he cannot honestly acknowledge his Father as such. Instead he should first go home, be reconciled with his brother, and then come to give his worship-offering (Mt. 5:23).

There is no doubt that the early Christians thought of

themselves, the Church, as a community of people rather than as a religious organization. Their life together, of course, had some patterns. Practical needs would have dictated some of these, as, for example, the appointment of the seven deacons to provide for the needs of the primitive Jerusalem community. Yet the organization of the earliest Christian communities was apparently quite diverse, and largely the result of providing for the circumstances that arose in each situation. Certain offices seem to have been common — that of the diaconate is a good example — but no uniform structure of community life existed in the first-century Church.

All the evidence of the New Testament literature, as well as that of other writings around the year 100 A.D., points to the fact that there were observable similarities among the early Christian communities. They all accepted the risen Lord and his Spirit in faith; they all worshipped the Father of our Lord Jesus Christ; they all celebrated the eucharistic breaking of bread; they all brought new members into their midst through the ritual of baptism; they all preached the Gospel; they all catechized their members according to the traditional witness of the Apostles. Moreover, a close bond of loving concern linked the disparate communities, and there seems to have been constant communication among them. Without any central organization or authority, the Christians of the various communities scattered throughout the Mediterranean world (and well beyond it) did have an awareness of belonging to one Church, one body of Christ.

There is, of course, a striking difference between the relatively unstructured Christianity of those early decades and the complex organization of the Church as we know it today. One must be careful not to pass a hasty value-judgment here, seeing either situation as the ideal externalization of the Church's life of faith and love. From a careful examination of the New Testament writings and their mirroring of the early Christian communities, what does emerge as a basic insight is this: While some organizational forms are necessary to help keep the Church unified and effective, these are of secondary importance and have validity only insofar as they give expression to and help support that which is of primary importance — the inner life of faith in the risen Christ. It is this life and the love that flows from it which most deeply form men and women into a Christian community.

A Sign of Promise

That such a community can exist is meant to be a sign of hope for men throughout history, hope that community among all men is a possibility. Despite the dissensions and prejudices and fears which find expression in bitter social divisions and even wars, the unity of mankind in justice and charity is not an unrealizable dream. This is what the Christian community is meant to speak to the world. Itself not yet a fully realized community but working toward that goal through the love Christians have for one another, the Church manifests to the world its own eschatological character and points thereby to the fact that all human history is eschatological, moving towards a goal of human fulfillment, a final situation in which all men will be truly one human family.

As a community of faith in the resurrection of Christ, the Church is meant to be a sign of promise to all men; promise, not just of human community, but of a community in shared life, unending life. The Holy Spirit, whom the risen Christ shares with his followers in the Church, and whom the early Christians experienced as the source of their communal consciousness and concern, is the life-giving Spirit. To the extent that men now share in this Spirit of the risen Christ, they live more fully. This Spirit-filled life they now have will flower into fullness of life as they pass through death into resurrection with Christ.

The Christian community, as it lives out the power of the Spirit in its midst, is meant to be a sign of the presence of that Spirit. As the epistle to the Ephesians explains (Eph.

1:13-14), the presence of the Spirit of Christ already vivifying men is the great promise that that life will go on unbroken and forever. What will go on towards fulfillment is much more than continuance in existence; it is personal life of the highest order, a sharing in the personal life of the Father and the Son themselves; it is a life of deep personal communication and community, between men and God and among men themselves. The Church is meant, in its historical career, to live increasingly that kind of life and to proclaim its reality to all men. To put it simply: The Church is meant to preach the Gospel of the risen Christ.

What, then, is the Church meant to be? What is its role in the salvation of mankind? And how necessary is that role? To one who reads with Christian faith the books of the New Testament, the answers to these questions are clear, although, as we have tried to point out, they must be found in somewhat different fashion by each generation of Christians, according to their own historical circumstances.

The Christian community is the body of Christ, the sacrament of his presence as the risen Lord. As such, the community's purpose is to be "the point of entry and contact" for the risen Christ as he continues among men his saving work. First and foremost, the Church exists to make present in human history the redeeming activity of Christ and of his Spirit.

But the Church is to do this "sacramentally," that is by speaking the mystery of Christ's presence through every aspect of its community life. Christians must verbally proclaim and explain the message of resurrection, but their entire life must also bear witness to their own faith in the message they preach. By their own unity with one another they are to bear witness to Christ's unifying power; by their individual and communal concern for all men they are to make clear that theirs is not an introverted and self-centered community, that their own unity in faith and love is directed towards the unification of all men.

Christians possess the risen Christ as friend and brother in order to share him with others. He — and he alone — is the savior. Only in union with him can men reach their destiny. This central tenet of Christian faith, so fundamental to the thought of the New Testament writers, makes clear the subordinate role of the Church. Whatever it does, it does with and for Christ and through the power of his Spirit. To it must apply the self-effacing words of John the Baptist: "He must increase, but I must decrease" (Jn. 3:30). This very self-effacement in order that Christ may be manifest is the glory and the fulfillment of the Church itself. The more fully Christ is brought to men, the more fully is the Church realizing its historical destiny.

Since the risen Christ is working in this fashion, making himself redemptively present to all men through the life and activity of the Christian people, there seems to be a necessity for the Church to last throughout history, but its necessity is that of Christ himself. There is a need for the Church, because there is an absolute need for the risen Christ himself. He is *the* sacrament of his Father's love; he is *the* prophet who brings to men his Father's word of love, for he is that word enfleshed.